"Leslie Vernick is a wise counselor, for she knows that in order to overcome depression, you have to fight. She is an experienced and thorough trainer who shares clearly and practically the necessary steps for getting into shape spiritually, emotionally, and physically in order to contend with depression."

> **Cynthia Heald,** international speaker;
> author of *A Woman's Journey to the Heart of God*

"An awesome book for women who have lost their joy and sense of direction in this demanding world...This book will teach women how to have heaven on earth and improve their quality of life."

> **Paris M. Finner-Williams, Ph.D.,** attorney and psychologist; coauthor of *Marital Secrets: Dating, Lies, Communication, and Sex*

"Leslie Vernick opens the lid to let in the light of truth and the sweet smell of hope. Her strong grip on biblical truth says, 'Come. I've been there too. I'll walk with you toward wholeness once again.'"

> **Virelle Kidder,** conference speaker,
> author of *Donkeys Still Talk*

"Leslie Vernick, with her professional expertise and personal experience, compassionately shows women how to stop pretending everything is okay, face their feelings with faith, correct wrong thinking, and bring peace to their panic."

> **Andrea Stephens,** author of *Stuff a Girl's Gotta Know; BRIO* magazine beauty editor; pastor's wife

"Leslie shows the Bible to be the absolute foundation of sound psychological principles. Her discussion of biological aspects of depression will hopefully help...truly address the spirit, mind, and body spheres of depression."

> **Karl Benzio, M.D.,** psychiatrist; Founder/Director of Lighthouse Network

"A clear and practical road map to help us through the pain, find our way out of the darkness, and even discover the surprising treasures hidden in our darkest days."

"Woven together to provide a message of hope and encouragement to those experiencing depression…without minimizing the pain and suffering depression can bring."

Defeating Depression

LESLIE VERNICK

HARVEST HOUSE PUBLISHERS

EUGENE, OREGON

Cover by Dugan Design Group, Bloomington, Minnesota

Cover photo © Susie Q. / Alamy; back-cover author photo © Sally Ullman Photography

The stories presented herein are true, though names and events have been changed to ensure confidentiality and protect each contributor's privacy.

ADVISORY

Readers are advised to consult with their physician or other medical practitioner before implementing any ideas that follow. This book is not intended to take the place of sound personal medical advice or to treat specific maladies. Neither the author nor the publisher assumes any liability for possible adverse consequences as a result of the information contained herein.

DEFEATING DEPRESSION
Copyright © 2005 by Leslie Vernick
Published by Harvest House Publishers
Eugene, Oregon 97402
www.harvesthousepublishers.com

Library of Congress Cataloging-in-Publication Data

Vernick, Leslie.
[Getting over the blues]
Defeating depression / Leslie Vernick.
   p. cm.
Originally published: Getting over the blues. Eugene, Or. : Harvest House Publishers, c2005.
ISBN 978-0-7369-2344-6 (pbk.)
1. Depression, Mental—Religious aspects—Christianity. 2. Depressed persons—Religious life.
3. Women—Religious life. I. Title.
BV4910.34.V47 2008
248.8'625—dc22

                                                                    2008020831

Printed in the United States of America

   09   10   11   12   13   14   15   16   / VP-SK /   10   9   8   7   6   5   4   3   2   1

Contents

Silent Battles

In my mind, dark specters
attempt to conquer me.
Subconscious wars I've waged
against these enemies.
At times I fight the battles
and think that I can win.
Other days, the darkness
just tells me to give in.

It's like I'm in a dream…
running in slow motion,
or floundering amidst
a deep and stormy ocean…
I reach out for a life raft,
but feel the anchor's weight.
If I don't release it,
drowning is my fate.

I'm trying to call out,
but cannot form the words.
Then screams become an echo
and only go unheard.
Trapped by walls of silence,
I issue my last plea—
"Oh, dear God in heaven,
please come and set me free."

ANONYMOUS

Walking out of Darkness into Light

We look for light, but all is darkness;
for brightness, but we walk in deep shadows.

ISAIAH 59:9

One summer's day while I was jumping waves in the ocean, a strong current sucked my legs out from under me. Without warning and against my will, the undertow carried me out to deep water. Frantically, I cried for help and my husband, Howard, rescued me. When I returned home, I made it my business to know what to do if I were ever again caught in an undertow.

Depression is like a powerful undertow that knocks you down or sucks you under. Furiously, we resist it, but we usually don't get anywhere. As with an undertow, when depression grabs us we feel too scared, too small, and too weak to fight against it.

I want you to know there *is* hope. You *can* effectively fight back and win over depression. How do I know? Because, in addition to working with depressed women as a Christian counselor, I have had to battle depression in my own life. I have learned and continue to practice the very things I want to help you learn.

Depression is so prevalent that one woman in eight will experience clinical depression in her lifetime. It is the number one cause of disability in women.[1] Many other women will periodically feel blue, down, sad, empty, and lost without experiencing the cluster of symptoms needed for a diagnosis of major depression. Most of these women will never receive appropriate help. Some women don't even realize that the symptoms they are experiencing are depression. Instead, they may complain of endless fatigue, various aches and pains, mental slowness or confusion, memory lapses, insomnia, irritability, sadness, and a nagging feeling of emptiness that won't go away.

I want to say this once and for all. Christians get depressed—sometimes very depressed. I have worked with many women who have experienced mild to severe depression. Most have become better. Some haven't. Those who have become better have learned to recognize the unhealthy patterns in their lives that contributed to their depression and worked hard to change them. Breaking free from the grasp of depression isn't as easy as TV commercials would like to suggest. Antidepressant medication, although a wonderful blessing for many, does not cure depression; medication only lessens the symptoms of depression.[2] We must learn how to recognize and fight this enemy of our joy. That is the reason for this book.

Much research has been done in the last 20 years on the psychology of women. This research is necessary and helpful for many reasons, one of which is that women are twice as likely to suffer from major depression as men are. Is this strictly due to physical differences and hormonal fluctuations, or is something more than biology at work?

One of the most consistent findings researchers have discovered is that women are relational beings who function best when they are well connected with others. Secular researchers who study the psychology of women have observed that *the* central organizing feature of a woman's development and sense of self is her connection to others.[3] We women define ourselves in the context of human relationships and base much of our sense of worth on our ability to make and maintain positive relationships. One of the essential elements to good mental health is having loving connections with others. An old Jewish proverb wisely reminds us, "Sticks in a bundle are unbreakable. Sticks alone can be broken by a child." The consequence of disconnection and broken relationships is often depression.

God's Word confirms the importance of fellowship and relationship (Romans 12:10). In addition to making us physical and spiritual beings, God made us relational beings. The two greatest commandments God gives us have to do with loving connection (Mark 12:28-31). We are to love him first and to love others deeply from the heart (1 Thessalonians 4:9-10; 1 Peter 1:22). We will find meaning, purpose, and identity through our connection with him and with others (see, for example, 2 Corinthians 5:16-21; 6:11-13; 8:5-7).

Listening to depressed women over a number of years, and their own explanations as to why they thought they were depressed, led me to look at depression through the lens of relationships. I've often discovered that beneath a woman's depression was a relationship difficulty that was denied, unresolved, or not being addressed in a godly way. I also found that women often struggled with depression because they and/or their loved ones lacked the skills to make or keep an authentic, supportive relationship with a loved one. Because a woman naturally defines herself in the context of her relationships, difficulties and losses in relationships affect her core identity and sense of well-being, thus making her more vulnerable to depression. Even when a woman's depression is physiologically based, depression always affects her relationship with herself, others, and God, which often triggers a downward spiral of guilt, blame, and self-hatred with negative thoughts, as well as sad, unhappy, and anxious feelings.

In *Defeating Depression,* I want to help you understand yourself, what factors contribute to getting depressed, and what you need to do differently so that you can combat your depression. I want you to begin to recognize the patterns of thinking and responding to life that make you vulnerable to becoming depressed in the first place. Each chapter will give you clear and simple information about the most common causes of depression and, most importantly, help you use that knowledge in a way that makes you better, stronger, and a more spiritually and emotionally mature person.

I have divided the book into three parts:

Part One: A Woman's Relationship with Herself[4]

Part Two: A Woman's Relationship with Others

Part Three: A Woman's Relationship with God

Throughout this book, I also want to help you know God better so that you will experience his love for you. Love is absolutely essential to our emotional, mental, physical, and spiritual health, and I want you to know and trust deep within your heart that no one loves you more than God does right now. I also want you to learn how to love others well and to be loved in return. I am not alone in wanting these things for you. God wants these things for you too.

At the end of each chapter, I will give you something specific to think about and something tangible for you to practice. As you read through this book, you may find it tempting to skip these applications. *Please* don't let yourself do that. You cannot learn to battle depression just by reading about it any more than you can learn how to dance, play the piano, or speak a foreign language simply by reading about it. True learning always involves acquiring information, applying it to real life, and repeatedly practicing it.

Think with me for a minute about how a baby first learns to walk. She doesn't just decide to walk one day and then get up and start walking. She first learns to pull herself up, and then she practices balancing herself. Only after she learns how to stand and balance does she tentatively take one or two small steps forward, still hanging onto the coffee table or her mommy's hand for security. She falls down many times. Fortunately for her, she doesn't tell herself that because she isn't able to do it perfectly the first time, she is a failure and can't do it. Intuitively a baby knows that learning always involves trial and error, and making mistakes is part of the process.

Because of your depression, you may not *feel* like reading the book or doing the application exercises. You may even tell yourself you can't. Sometimes we make an effort, but when we fall down, we tell ourselves we're a failure because we didn't do it right or perfectly the first time. That's not true. You must learn to give yourself credit for taking a step to get better, even if in the process you fall down.

The practice exercises at the end of each chapter are called "First Steps" and will help you focus on one area at a time to work on and strengthen so that you will learn the skills to effectively fight your depression. Some parts may be easy for you. Perhaps you already know how to do them. Great, you're one step ahead. Other exercises you may be tempted to skip, thinking they won't really make a difference. Again, please don't do that. Each step is designed to give you a skill or a muscle you will need to fight depression. Don't think any one step is insignificant or unimportant. They all work together to give you the physical, emotional, spiritual, mental, and interpersonal strength you need to fight your depression—and fight to win.

If all you can do right now is read one page, then start there. Take one small step at a time. Hang on to God and watch how one small step can lead to the next one and the next one. When you fall down (and you will), accept falling as a normal part of your learning process. You had that attitude when you first learned to walk, and your ability to get up and try again is what enabled you to master walking and eventually the harder skills of running, skipping, and jumping.

To encourage you in the process, I've asked other women who have battled depression to share in their own words some of the steps they have taken and the things they have learned and found helpful along the way. I hope their words will inspire you and help you realize that *you are not alone,* and you can get better too.

I'm often asked, "How long will it take until I feel better?" The desire for quick relief is understandable. The answer depends upon a number of factors. If you are taking antidepressant medication and involved in individual counseling, you should begin to feel some relief in about five to eight weeks. However, if your depression has been chronic or recurrent, you know that feeling better may be temporary.

In order to gain the ability to fight future bouts of depression, you must begin to see yourself, God, and others differently. You must learn healthier and more truthful ways of thinking, feeling, and living with yourself and with others. These skills are not usually mastered easily or quickly, and they take repeated practice, as with any other new skill, in order for them to feel a natural part of who you are.

The ideal way to apply this book would be to use it in conjunction with a Christian counselor and a medical doctor (if medication is necessary) so that you have a treatment plan tailored for your individual needs. If you are experiencing severe depression, you need extra outside help. You would not attempt to deal with heart disease or diabetes on your own. Don't place an unrealistic burden on yourself. If you're unable to seek professional help for whatever reason and are reading this book, please promise yourself that if you become overwhelmed or are tempted to give up on life, you will immediately call for help. You can call your pastor, Crisis Intervention (that phone number is usually found in the blue pages of your phone book), or go to your local hospital emergency room.

I have been praying for you as I have written this book. I know depression feels like a brutal stranger choking the life out of you. It is tempting to believe you are helpless to fight it, that it's hopeless to try, and you're worthless anyway—so why bother? These are a few of the lies that I address in this book. It is my prayer that you will have the rich experience of knowing God as your Comforter, Healer, Redeemer, and Restorer. He wants you to know that you are *not* worthless, things are *not* hopeless, and that you are *not* helpless. You are *not* alone. He will help you fight this battle!

He reached down from on high and took hold of me;
he drew me out of deep waters.
He rescued me from my powerful enemy,
from my foes, who were too strong for me.
Psalm 18:16-17

Part One

A Woman's Relationship with Herself

What Is Happening to Me?

My heart is stricken and withered like grass,
so that I forget to eat my bread. Because of the
sound of my groaning my bones cling to my skin.
PSALM 102:4-5 NKJV

Puffy red blotches covered Mary's creamy porcelain skin. As she spoke, tears ran down her nose. Embarrassed, she quickly brushed them away. "I don't know what is wrong with me! I'm not myself. I used to be a capable person, but I can't seem to do the simplest things anymore. I cry at the drop of a hat. I can't sleep. I don't even enjoy my kids."

I asked Mary how long she had been feeling this way. She told me that over the past few months she had noticed a gradual change in herself. At first she felt sad, then empty and sort of lost, and finally she grew more and more numb. She wasn't sure why. "I don't care about anything anymore. Am I going crazy? I'm so scared. I want to feel like my old self again."

"No, Mary, you're not crazy," I responded. "I think you're depressed. I'm glad you've come for help."

What Is Depression?

Depression is a physical, mental, spiritual, and emotional response to something that is wrong. The million-dollar question is, "What is wrong?"—and sometimes there are no simple answers. We will tackle this question of *what is wrong* and the causes and triggers of depression more thoroughly in chapter 2. For now, understand that most often what is wrong is multifaceted. One thing is certain, though. Whatever the cause, depression can be devastating and impacts our whole person, as well as those we love.

Once Mary understands that the symptoms she experiences have a name—major depression—it is crucial that she also takes the time to decipher what her depression is telling her. If she doesn't give her symptoms the attention they deserve, she will not be able to identify the underlying problem(s), learn the skills, or make the changes she needs to make that will allow her to be less vulnerable to depressive episodes in the future.

First, let's look at the symptoms of depression.

How Do I Know I Am Depressed?

For many women, depression is a generic word we use to describe how we feel when we're down in the dumps, stressed-out, overwhelmed, hurt, or sad. Many of us have had bad days or even a bad couple of days, but then we start to feel better and our *depressed mood* passes. Those who lean toward a melancholy temperament or struggle with bouts of depressed feelings for a few days will benefit greatly from reading this book and practicing the exercises in it. Doing so can help you prevent your symptoms from becoming more severe or lasting longer.

Unfortunately, there are no blood tests to determine if you are depressed. Below is a general checklist of the physical, emotional, mental, and spiritual manifestations of depression that most physicians and mental health professionals would use to determine if a person was clinically depressed. As you read through all the symptoms below, place a check mark next to the symptoms that describe you. If you are averse to writing directly in your book, make a photocopy of this page and the next page to mark.

Physical Symptoms of Depression
- ☐ Chronic aches and pains that are not explained by other medical conditions
- ☐ Sleep disturbances (waking early, insomnia, extreme fatigue)
- ☐ Not taking care of your appearance the way you used to
- ☐ Eating disturbances (excessive overeating, loss of appetite and weight)
- ☐ Loss of sexual interest
- ☐ Low energy, feeling of heaviness, lethargy, slowed speech

Emotional Symptoms of Depression
- ☐ Feeling guilty
- ☐ Feeling worthless and undeserving of anything good
- ☐ Feeling disappointed in oneself
- ☐ Feeling sad for no apparent reason, excessive crying
- ☐ Feeling numb, as though the plug has been pulled out and there is no "life" in you
- ☐ Loss of interest in things previously enjoyed
- ☐ Feeling hopeless or pessimistic about the future
- ☐ Irritability, restlessness, agitation
- ☐ Anxiety, possibly with panic symptoms

Mental Symptoms of Depression
- ☐ Inability to concentrate
- ☐ Can't make decisions the way you used to
- ☐ Recurrent thoughts of death and/or suicide
- ☐ Difficulty thinking and remembering
- ☐ Negative view of self, others, and life
- ☐ Attitude of "it doesn't matter" and "I don't matter"

Spiritual Symptoms of Depression

☐ Morbid preoccupation with faults and/or failures

☐ Excessive guilt, with no relief through prayer and forgiveness

☐ Hopelessness

☐ Feeling abandoned or rejected by God

☐ Lack of meaning or purpose in life; sense of emptiness

☐ Loss of interest in spiritual things that were once meaningful (prayer, Bible reading, church, worship, and/or Christian music)

Relational Symptoms of Depression

☐ Withdrawal from friends, church, work colleagues, and family

Now that you have checked all the symptoms that apply to you, go back over your check marks and evaluate whether you experience each checked symptom in a mild, moderate, or severe way. Write your answer down next to your check mark. As you do this, also note about how long you have had each symptom. Has it been a few days? Weeks? Months? Years?

Here's an example:

☑ Feeling worthless and undeserving of anything good—*moderate intensity, felt this way all my life*

After you have finished, step back and take a big picture perspective. Look at how many symptoms you checked, how severe your symptoms are, and how long they have lasted. Are your check marks more densely clustered in one category over another? Evaluating your symptoms and answering these questions are important keys that can begin to unlock the mystery of your depression. Your unique responses begin to give you some clues as to what might be wrong.

Every symptom will not apply to everyone, even if you are seriously depressed. You may only have a few of these symptoms and still be depressed, especially if your symptoms have persisted longer than two weeks and are moderate to severe. If you answered yes to some of the questions and your symptoms have lasted longer than two weeks, I highly recommend that you make an appointment to see a Christian counselor for a professional opinion. You may also want to take a confidential depression screening test online through The National Mental Health Association. (You will find them at www.nmha.org.)

Professionals consider many factors when making the diagnosis of clinical depression. Sometimes it isn't easy to diagnose because there are other problems that can coexist with depression. For example, some women are depressed but don't realize it because they also struggle with an anxiety disorder, drug or alcohol abuse, marital problems, or a physical illness that can mask a coexisting depression. Some of the signs professionals look for to ascertain whether someone is depressed or not are how long the symptoms have persisted, how severe they are, and whether the person is having trouble functioning at home or at work. The presence of suicidal and/or self-destructive thoughts is a clear indicator of depression.

Some symptoms of depression are easier to notice than others. Women have described feeling hopeless, sad, numb, or anxious. They find no pleasure in things they once enjoyed. Others say they can't concentrate, make decisions, or think clearly. When depression is severe, a person finds it hard to do the basics of self-care, such as shower, eat, or get dressed, and thoughts of death or suicide are common.

Listen to how some women who were depressed felt:

> *I lost interest in everything. It was difficult for me even to do the things I enjoyed the most. I also withdrew from everyone. I didn't want to talk on the phone or do anything with others. It became a chore to go to work. I didn't want to get out of bed. On the weekends I preferred to stay in my pajamas and remain in bed for as long as possible. Even the easiest things became chores.*

It happened so slowly that I didn't even know it until one day when I couldn't get out of bed and I couldn't stop crying. It was then I knew I needed help. ~Donna

I had been sad for a long time, but this was way past sad. I had trouble getting out of bed. I was extremely tired and exhausted. I cried constantly. Yes, I did have reasons to be sad and to cry, but I couldn't stop crying. I had trouble deciding what to wear and would break down and cry over little everyday decisions I never used to think twice about making. ~Cindy

It is difficult to describe the state of depression to someone else, especially if that person has never experienced it. The severity differs from feeling like something is just not right in the world to feeling like nothing is right in the world. The range of emotion is anywhere from sad to suicidal. I think I have experienced all of these. Depression can be utterly debilitating and it can be deadly. It is soul destroying. ~Cheryl

We can all experience these feelings from time to time, but to lesser degrees and for less time. It is the intensity and duration of these symptoms that may indicate you are experiencing a more serious depression.

Seeing yourself in some of these symptoms may feel frightening to you. Many times we don't want to admit that we're slipping over the edge of a steep cliff and we can't stop it. Maybe you can identify with Diane or Gwen:

Intellectually, I think I knew I was depressed far sooner than I chose to admit, but I wasn't of the mindset that depression was actually a real issue. Even though I could answer yes to most, if not all, of the questions on depression surveys, I still wouldn't and/or couldn't admit it to myself, let alone someone else. ~Diane

During my first incident with depression, I didn't initially label the symptoms as depression. I had several physical and emotional symptoms that I later realized were characteristic of depression: difficulty concentrating, memory lapses, sadness, loss of interest in previously enjoyed activities, frequent thoughts of suicide or wishing I were dead, fatigue, hopelessness, and weight gain. I knew I was not my normal self but did not want to consider the possibility of depression. However, the most current episode of depression was more recognizable. Although it was not as severe, I was more aware of the characteristics that had accompanied the previous episode. And yet there is still the desire to not label it as depression and, consequently, a denial of the symptoms.   *~ Gwen*

Don't Ignore Your Depressive Symptoms

God has led you to read this book for a reason, and he wants you to get the help you need to get better. If you are experiencing some of these symptoms, especially if they have lasted longer than two weeks, please don't ignore them, hoping you'll get better or they'll go away on their own. Psychiatrist Dr. Michael Lyles says, "The impact of untreated depression on the brain is enormous. There is an area of the brain that generates new brain cells, a sort of neuronal 'greenhouse' called the hippocampal gyrus. Untreated depression has been associated with irreversible damage and atrophy to this area, thus depriving the brain of the ability to replace aging and dying cells." He also adds, "The brain effects of untreated depression can affect other organs of the body."[1]

In addition to the physical consequences of untreated depression, there are serious emotional and relational consequences. Untreated depression accounts for 10 to 13 percent of all suicides. A depressed woman may resort to self-medication through alcohol, drug abuse, or other addictions in an attempt to ease her pain. Divorce, abuse, job loss, and financial ruin can often be traced back to untreated depression.

Listen to Sarah's experience:

> *My resentment of the lack of support and friendship with my husband has taken me to many, many dark and lonely places in addiction. Resentment and fear in general have fueled these addictions. I have sought to relieve my depression and lost dreams through alcohol, cigarettes, and food.*   *~Sarah*

If you recognize several of the symptoms of depression in yourself, please make an appointment with your medical doctor for a checkup and evaluation in addition to seeing a Christian counselor. You may have one of several medical conditions that mimic the symptoms of depression and that medication will easily remedy. One of the most common and underdiagnosed conditions for women is hypothyroidism (an underactive thyroid), which is detected through a simple blood test. If your doctor rules out a medical condition and thinks you are depressed, he or she may recommend that you begin taking some antidepressant medication.

Many Christian women have ambivalent feelings about antidepressant medications as well as about personal counseling. They may see such things as yet more evidence of personal failure. Or they may have been told that with enough faith they wouldn't need those things. For others, the financial cost of the medication and counseling are prohibitive, especially if they don't have medical insurance. Some women fear that taking medicine will make them feel like a zombie or that they will become addicted to their medication.

Here are the words of some women who struggled with this issue:

> *I was leery about taking medication because I did not know if it was biblical. Once I received peace from God that it was okay, I still struggled on and off for seven months in my commitment to taking medication. My pride did not want to accept the fact that I needed to be dependent on something in addition to God. I felt weak.*   *~Stacy*

The first time the medication was prescribed, I didn't get it filled right away. I really felt like I had failed. I was embarrassed...and ashamed. It even took me awhile to begin taking it once I did finally get the prescription filled. I made sure I took it to a different pharmacy than the one where I got all of the other family medications. I was so afraid someone (even my husband) would find out. There are only a few people who know I'm taking it.   *~Diane*

We will talk more about how depression affects our body, and the pros and cons of taking medication, later in chapters 2 and 3. For certain types of depression, medication is a necessary part of the healing process.

Types of Depression

Depression doesn't look the same for everyone, and sometimes it is useful in making sense of your particular depression to understand how mental health professionals classify the most common types of depression.

Major Depression—Clinical Depression

Major depression is the most familiar kind of depression, where a person has a depressed mood and a decreased ability to go about normal life. It characteristically manifests itself in a loss of pleasure in previously enjoyed activities and feelings of hopelessness or worthlessness that are present for at least two weeks. Major depression may come back again once you've experienced it. That is why it is important to recognize and minimize your particular vulnerabilities so that you will lessen the possibility of recurrence.

I lost interest in things I usually enjoy. I had a lack of physical energy and didn't want to do anything. I felt sad, discouraged, and hopeless.   *~Anna*

Chronic Depression—Dysthymia

Chronic depression may go undiagnosed because it is so long-standing that a woman often believes her experience is just how she is. Chronic depression has the same symptoms as major depression, but they are less severe, usually enabling a woman to function in an empty sort of way. In order for the diagnosis of chronic depression to be made, a person must experience the symptoms of depression for at least two years, without a break lasting longer than two months. Such women can also experience major depression at the same time, making it a double depression.

> *I have suffered most of my life with a mild form of depression. I experienced a lethargic, indifferent, groggy, and numb state in which I could function and carry on, but with no enthusiasm. About five times in the last 20 years I got worse. I was crying all the time and would withdraw and isolate myself from outside activities, preferring to be alone.*   *~Brenda*

Bipolar Depression

Bipolar depression is less common and used to be called manic depression. It is characterized by cycling mood swings with lows and highs that can last from several days to months. Euphoric and/or irritable feelings, reckless acting out or spending (not normally characteristic of the person), and a decreased need for sleep characterize the highs and mania phase and, without medical intervention, often worsens to a psychotic state. Untreated, a person with bipolar depression has a 20 to 25 percent risk of suicide.[2]

If you've ever experienced a manic episode, or a decreased need for sleep combined with a high daytime energy level, be sure to disclose this to your physician, even if you are currently only feeling depressed. Your doctor needs this information so that he or she can correctly prescribe the right medicine or combination of medicines for your condition.

Seasonal Affective Disorder (SAD)

This year in Pennsylvania, winter was long, unusually cloudy, and harsh. Toward the end of January, calls began pouring in to my office from women who were feeling depressed. SAD is related to a lack of sunlight and an associated buildup of the sleep hormone, melatonin. Women are more prone to SAD than men are, and the most effective treatment is light therapy to simulate sunlight. My husband and I turned down a great job offer in overcast Oregon because of my need for regular sunshine. One of my clients always scheduled a two-week vacation in a sunny climate in the middle of January to boost her mood.

Hormone-Related Depression

Women face particular vulnerabilities to depression because of the ways their bodies work. About 20 percent of women will experience some postpartum depression, and it can occur anytime throughout the first year after delivery. Hormonal fluctuations that occur during a woman's menstrual cycle may, for some women, cause more serious physical, cognitive, and emotional upsets than are usual and are related to premenstrual syndrome (PMS), or premenstrual dysphoric disorder (PMDD), as well as some of the problems women experience during menopause. A drop in estrogen levels causes these mood changes, and where severe, medical intervention may be necessary.

Vickki understood her depression better when she realized that it began after her child was born:

> When I was first diagnosed as depressed, I felt relief. WHEW! This is what's wrong. THIS is why life is so hard. I sought a counselor specializing in depression because although I have a strong faith in God, I was unable to hear him anymore. Nothing made sense, the Bible was dry, and I couldn't hear what I needed to get from my reading and prayer time. As I looked back over the past

years I felt grief. I realized I had been suffering from post-
partum depression that went undiagnosed for four years
before I got help. Life has been crazy since the day I gave
birth.   *~ Vickki*

Remember, not all types of depression look the same or have the same causes. The symptoms are on a continuum and may range from quite mild to very severe. Don't dismiss or minimize your symptoms because they aren't disabling you yet. A sprained ankle isn't as serious as a broken leg and a broken leg isn't as serious as a severed one. But in each case, the person requires wise and specialized care in order to maximize healing and to minimize further chances of damage, disability, or even death.

God cares about how you feel. He has compassion for your suffering. He wants to help you (Hebrews 2:16-18).

How God Sees the Person Who Is Depressed

Much more about our relationship with God will be covered in subsequent chapters, and especially in chapters 10 and 11, but for the moment I want you to know a few things that God says to you. In your present state these verses may sound hollow to you. For now, try to read them out loud to yourself and listen to them. Don't worry or feel bad if you find them hard to believe.

Depression screams, "God has forgotten me."
God says, "I have not forgotten you."

Those who suffer can feel as if God has forgotten them. The psalmist often describes those feelings, and even Jesus experienced God's absence when dying on the cross. Although our feelings are powerful, they don't always tell us the truth. For example, listen to the dialogue between God and Israel in these verses:

> Yet Jerusalem says: "The LORD has deserted us; the Lord
> has forgotten us" (Isaiah 49:14 NLT).

God responds:

> Never! Can a mother forget her nursing child? Can she
> feel no love for a child she has borne? But even if that
> were possible, I would not forget you! See, I have written
> your name on my hand. Ever before me is a picture of
> Jerusalem's walls in ruins (Isaiah 49:15-16 NLT).

In these verses Israel struggled between believing what God said
and her own subjective feelings—and so do we. Here are a few passages of Scripture reassuring us that God sees and knows our pain:

> My eyes grow weak with sorrow; they fail because of all
> my foes. Away from me, all you who do evil, for the LORD
> has heard my weeping. The LORD has heard my cry for
> mercy; the LORD accepts my prayer (Psalm 6:7-9).

> But you, O God, do see trouble and grief; you consider
> it to take it in hand. The victim commits himself to you;
> you are the helper of the fatherless (Psalm 10:14).

Depression screams, "No one cares!"
God says, "I care about you."

God is not a passive observer of our suffering. He entered our
world and knows what life is like. The Bible tells us that Jesus knew
heartache and sorrow (Isaiah 53:3).

> In my distress I called to the LORD; I cried to my God for
> help. From his temple he heard my voice; my cry came
> before him, into his ears (Psalm 18:6).

> A Message from the high and towering God, who lives
> in Eternity, whose name is Holy: "I live in the high and
> holy places, but also with the low-spirited, the spirit-
> crushed. And what I do is put a new spirit in them, get
> them up and on their feet again" (Isaiah 57:15 MSG).

Depression screams, "You're all alone."
God says, "I will not abandon you."

When Lazarus died, his sisters, Mary and Martha, were heartbroken. Not only had their beloved brother died, but their dearest friend, Jesus, didn't seem to care about their need (see John 11 for the story). When they informed him that Lazarus was sick, Jesus didn't respond and Lazarus died. Perhaps Mary and Martha thought Jesus was too busy with more important matters, healing others or teaching in the synagogue, to be available in their time of need. When we're desperate and God feels far away and doesn't seem to hear our cry for help, we feel the same way.

As we read the story we know, however, that Jesus *did* care. The Bible says, "Jesus loved Martha and her sister and Lazarus. Yet, when he heard that Lazarus was sick, he stayed where he was two more days" (John 11:5-6). Although Mary and Martha didn't know it, Jesus knew exactly what he was doing and why he didn't come immediately to meet their cry for help. He felt their grief and shed tears, even knowing he would raise Lazarus from the dead.

It is hard to figure out what God is doing much of the time. He knows we don't always understand the big picture and that when life gets difficult we become filled with fear, doubt, and even anger. He reassures us in those times that he is near, even if we don't *feel* his presence.

Here are a few verses to remind us again and again of that important truth:

> The LORD is close to the brokenhearted and saves those who are crushed in spirit (Psalm 34:18).

> Even though I walk through the valley of the shadow of death, I will fear no evil, for you are with me (Psalm 23:4).

> I am convinced that nothing can ever separate us from his love. Death can't, and life can't. The angels can't, and the demons can't. Our fears for today, our worries about

tomorrow, and even the powers of hell can't keep God's love away. Whether we are high above the sky or in the deepest ocean, nothing in all creation will ever be able to separate us from the love of God that is revealed in Christ Jesus our Lord (Romans 8:38-39 NLT).

Depression screams, "No one hears me."
God says, "Talk to me."

When Jesus finally arrived at Mary and Martha's home four days after Lazarus had been in the tomb, you can imagine how upset and hurt they were. Martha, the first to greet Jesus, blurted out her true feelings: "Lord, if you had been here, my brother would not have died" (John 11:21). I can almost hear her gasp as she realized she was scolding Jesus for neglecting them. Quickly she recovers her religious language and adds, "But I know that even now God will give you whatever you ask" (verse 22). Jesus didn't bristle at Martha for her honest talk. Instead, he invited her into a dialogue with him about what happened and how she felt.

I see the same thing when I read Job questioning God as he pours out his complaint again and again, looking for answers to *why* his whole life was falling apart (Job 10). Jeremiah, the weeping prophet, angrily accuses God of being unfair and cruel (Lamentations 3), and the psalmist regularly pours out his heartfelt emotions and thoughts to God. He said,

> I cried out to God for help; I cried out to God to hear me. When I was in distress, I sought the Lord; at night I stretched out untiring hands and my soul refused to be comforted (Psalm 77:1-2).

> Why, O LORD, do you reject me and hide your face from me? From my youth I have been afflicted and close to death; I have suffered your terrors and am in despair. Your wrath has swept over me; your terrors have destroyed me. All day long they surround me like a flood; they have completely engulfed me. You have taken my companions

and loved ones from me; the darkness is my closest friend
(Psalm 88:14-18).

For Mary and Martha, Jeremiah, Job, the psalmist, and all of us
who seek God in the depths of despair, God always hears our cries.
He answers us by drawing us into deeper awareness of who he is and
a greater capacity to know him.

"Trust in him at all times, O people; pour out your hearts to him,
for God is our refuge" (Psalm 62:8).

Facing Your Pain and Problems

Something to Think About

Recently my daughter, Amanda, needed to buy another car. Her car's engine died. It was an expensive lesson in learning to pay attention to the warning lights on the dashboard. Over the past year, Amanda noticed that her "check oil" light would flash, but she reasoned to herself that because her car ran and she was a college student who had little money for extras, she could ignore the light for the time being. That is, until the car stopped running.

Similarly, one of my clients told me, "I get busy so I don't have to look at myself. I'm afraid to see my pain, my sadness, my anger, and my guilt for everything. I'm afraid to see the wrong things I've done and the wrong things done to me. It's terrifying. I shut down."

Like the lights on the dashboard of a car, our emotions are often the first warning signals that something is wrong and we'd better pay attention.

Just as my daughter tried to avoid the reality of her car problems by ignoring her oil light flashing, my client viewed painful feelings as an enemy to be avoided at all costs. But her pain was trying to warn her of deeper problems. Just as physical pain is a signal that something is wrong with our bodies, emotional pain is a warning that there are deeper problems brewing. If we don't pay attention to what our pain is trying to tell us, the pain starts to get louder and louder until we either pay attention or break down.

Psychologist Dan Allender said, "Pain is not the enemy, denial is." Ask yourself this question: Do you think your depression has anything to do with avoiding something that is painful in your life?

Something to Do

To put what you are learning into practice, I want you to grab a piece of paper or, if you prefer, purchase a special journal, and begin talking to God. Write out your true thoughts and feelings the way the psalmist did. Admit them to yourself and to God. Do this every time you feel upset—even if it's about the smallest thing. Don't allow busyness, fear, or shame stop you from taking this first step.

If you have trouble getting started, read through some of the psalms mentioned in this chapter or Lamentations 3, where Jeremiah angrily pours his heart out to God. God doesn't want you to pretend you're fine or that nothing's bothering you. Talk to him honestly about what's wrong and how you feel, even if you wish you weren't feeling that way.

It takes courage to admit how you feel to yourself and to God. It also takes courage to be able to acknowledge the problems behind your pain. To heal, we must start to pay attention to what our feelings are saying. But here is one word of caution. Dallas Willard wisely warns in his book *Renovations of the Heart*, "Feelings are, with a few exceptions, good servants. But they are disastrous masters."[3]

After writing in your journal, finish up by reading aloud this important truth: *God is always with me, even if I don't feel him right now.* This is what he says to you, "Don't panic. I'm with you. There's no need to fear for I'm your God. I'll give you strength. I'll help you. I'll hold you steady, keep a firm grip on you" (Isaiah 41:10 MSG).

What Causes Depression?

Why am I discouraged?
Why so sad?
I will put my hope in God!
I will praise him again—
My Savior and my God!
PSALM 42:5-6 NLT

Depression, as we have already seen, is not a simple problem nor does it have a single origin. People who boil down the reasons for depression to one underlying root cause usually fall into two extremes. One group sees depression solely as a spiritual problem. Although many people in this category are well meaning Christians, they speak passionately about things they know little about. As a result, they often carelessly wound depressed women. Like Job's friends, they offer simplistic explanations to life's difficulties, only adding more pain to the sufferer's already full plate. They may say things like, "Depression is a sin or a choice." Other women have been chastised with, "If you really trusted God, you wouldn't get depressed." These statements put a tremendous amount of blame and pressure on a person for not only feeling depressed, but also for not having enough faith to prevent getting depressed in the first place.

Jill tearfully approached me during a women's retreat. "Do you have a few minutes to talk?" she asked. I invited her to my room after lunch, where she began to share her heart. "I want to know God better," she said, "but I don't know how to find him. I know my hope is supposed to be in him, but there is so much garbage in my life that I feel like I want to die. My marriage stinks, my parents don't really care about me or the kids, and I feel so lonely at church. Even at this retreat, I feel all alone. No one knows the real me." As I listened, I noticed that Jill exhibited many of the symptoms of depression I listed in the last chapter. When I suggested that perhaps part of her problem was that she was depressed and that she had some real issues in her life she needed to face, her head dropped low and she whispered, "I feel so ashamed and guilty for feeling this way. If only I had more faith."

When a person concludes that the only cause of depression is spiritual, she feels tremendous guilt and shame. She may think to herself, *God must be disappointed in me because I can't climb out of this hole I'm in. Why don't I have enough trust or enough faith to find my way out of this deep pit?* If her physician recommends antidepressant medication, she usually refuses to take it. She fears she will be "depending on medicine instead of God to make her better." Depression definitely has spiritual components, which we will begin to look at later on in this chapter and examine more fully throughout the book; however, spiritual reasons are not the sole cause.

On the other side of the spectrum are those who define depression as purely a physical disease. They often say, "You have a chemical imbalance" or "runaway hormones" or "stinky genetics." Proponents of this viewpoint see depression as a physical problem such as heart disease or diabetes. But even physical illnesses have emotional, mental, and spiritual components.

For example, my brother was recently diagnosed with coronary artery disease. A twinge of pain shooting down his arm during a golf game gave him pause in his busy life, and he made an appointment with his family doctor as soon as he got home. Just like depression, the pain in his arm told him something was wrong. "What's wrong?" is always the critical question we must answer. After some tests his doctor told him he had three blocked arteries. He would need stents inserted in his arteries in order to restore adequate blood flow. Like the flashing oil light in a car, the pain in his arm was a good thing.

We were thankful he took the time to pay attention and look for what was wrong.

But was it enough for his doctor to simply relieve his pain and open his clogged arteries? Or was it equally important to find out why, at 43, he had three clogged arteries in the first place? Was there a family history of coronary heart disease? Was his diet healthy and did he participate in aerobic exercise? Was he a smoker? How did he handle his emotions, such as anger, and how did he deal with stress and relationship difficulties? These questions all shed light onto someone's vulnerability to heart disease. For my brother to adequately deal with his heart problem, in addition to having his arteries opened, he must also examine his lifestyle and make changes where necessary. His physical pain was alleviated with the medical procedure. However, for his overall health and continued well-being, it was crucial that he address other issues that possibly caused his heart disease to begin with.

Defining depression as an illness or disease that can be cured simply with medicine is misleading. A woman experiencing depression must not only work toward *feeling* better, but she must also realize that part of *getting* better involves looking at her overall lifestyle. Through this process she learns to identify and change the patterns that may have contributed to her becoming depressed in the first place.

Depression Is a Complex Affliction

Depression is a multifaceted condition, rooted in both our inner life *and* our bodies, often triggered by situational and relational difficulties. No single cause can be pinpointed as the origin of this problem. Depression begins and grows out of a complex interplay between our bodies (biological factors), our minds (the way we think and look at things), our habits (our personality style and patterns we have developed for coping with people and life's stresses), interpersonal factors (our relationships with others, past and present), and spiritual problems (sinful responses, faulty teaching or under-standing regarding God and his character, and a loss of purpose or meaning to life). Richard O'Connor, a psychologist who has written extensively on depression, says,

> I realize now that no simple, single-factor theory of depression will ever work. Depression is partly in our genes, partly in our childhood experience, partly in our way of thinking, partly in our brains, partly in our ways of handling our emotions. It affects our whole being.[1]

Read some insights from women who understand the multi-faceted nature of depression:

> *I had very poor coping skills, lack of responsibility, over-sensitivity, anger, lots of failure, a poor marriage, a poor relationship with my parents—I could go on! I think that is why I struggled with the decision to take medicine—because I knew there were some things I needed to work on that medicine would not cure. However, the medi-cine helped me to climb out of the black hole I was in so I was actually able to work on things.* ~ Rebecca

> *I think what contributed to my depression were alcoholic parents, chronic shame, and a poor self-image. Also, there were a string of losses, deaths throughout my life, including my mother and a miscarriage. Hormonal changes after each pregnancy affected me. Draining relationships, mar-ital problems, and trying to live in the skin of a different personality type for many years nearly sucked the life out of me. I have relatives who were depressed, so maybe I have an inherited trait for it too.* ~ Diane

> *Some of the things that contributed to my depression were a lifelong pattern of negative thinking, a difficult*

situation that was not improving, an inability to see God's perspective on my situation, a lack of trust in God's love and his power to change me and others, a superficial relationship with God and a habitual way of coping with potential or real pain.   ~Gwen

To understand how all these factors build together to shape a significant depressive episode, let me share Tina's story with you.

At work Tina was accused of undermining her boss's authority and was terminated from a job she loved. Although she always knew there was a personality clash between them, Tina felt horrified, her emotions quickly tumbled out of control, and she became full of fear. While driving home she told herself that this was the worst thing that had ever happened to her and that she would never be able to find another job. She thought everyone would be talking about her and she would lose all her work friends. She imagined herself homeless and living on the streets. As soon as she walked in the door of her apartment, she crawled into bed and stayed there—for days. Distraught and anxious, Tina couldn't eat or sleep. She became physically ill. Ashamed for being fired, Tina withdrew from her friends and family and wouldn't answer her phone. She felt helpless and was angry with God for allowing her unfair termination. Her spiritual, mental, and emotional response to her job loss and unfair treatment affected her physically, and she became extremely depressed.

Tina's story illustrates that depression is often set in motion by a traumatic event or difficult loss in life. As we can clearly see in Tina's situation, however, her initial depressed feelings gained momentum by her feelings of shame and habits of thinking and coping with loss. We may not be able to change our heredity or control many difficult situations that life throws our way, but we can and must begin to look at how we process our troubles and cope with them—or don't. That understanding will teach us how to handle not only life's problems, but also our runaway thoughts and emotions in a way that God says is good and right.

Life is often difficult. When we consistently fail to handle trials the way God teaches us in his Word, depression is often the result. Psychologist David J. McKay says, "Because of the Fall [when Adam and Eve disobeyed God], our behaviors are maladaptive, our thoughts are irrational, our biology is flawed, and our perceptions are distorted. It is not surprising that our emotions have also been disturbed by the Fall."[2]

Human beings are wonderfully complex. We have a body and a spirit, a material and an immaterial side. In looking for the cause of depression, it is important that we understand that we are not merely victims of something that "happens to us." What is going on in our heart as well as in our bodies has something to do with why we become depressed, as shown in the diagram.

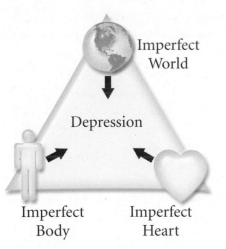

Research shows that loss is one of the most significant external precipitants to depression. Learning to recognize your losses, especially those that are less obvious, is critical so that we grieve our losses in the turbulence of life's storms while still holding on to God.

Loss Is Often a Contributing Factor in Depression

Life is full of losses. Like Tina, we may lose our job through unfair cutbacks, personality clashes, or downturns in the economy. Other women lose their spouses from death or divorce. We can lose our health or our positions of authority at work or at church. We can feel depressed even when we lose intangible things, such as our reputation or our dream of a happy marriage or something else we hoped for. Losses come in all sizes, big and small, and none of us escape.

> *I lost my grandmother at an early age, and she was like my mother. My manager at my first job committed suicide, and I had looked up to her very much. My mom and dad were divorced when I was two years old, and he never had anything to do with me. My mom's second husband was killed in an automobile accident when I was nine years old, and then two days later my mother gave birth to my brother. We then moved to a different state away from my family, and my mom dated a drug addict and alcoholic for eight years. I think those losses have a lot to do with why I hate being alone and easily get depressed.*   *~ Tammy*

Samantha became depressed after she failed to get into a graduate program for her Ph.D. Her dream was to become someone important and have an impact on others. A Ph.D. was her ticket. When it looked as though it wasn't going to happen, she lost her dream and her hope for her future quickly faded. She became sad and hurt and angry. She told herself that her life didn't matter and all her previous training and schooling was a waste of time. She didn't want to switch gears and find something else to do; she wanted to pursue her dream. If she couldn't do that, she concluded her life did not matter. She didn't matter. Nothing mattered!

Healthy people face loss with deep sadness, even some anger, but they don't experience a reduction of self-esteem and feelings of worthlessness so characteristic of depression. It's important that we not confuse depression with the normal grieving process, although some of the symptoms (such as insomnia, sadness, and helpless feelings) may overlap.

Many of us want to take a shortcut around the pain of our loss instead of feeling the pain and going through it. Depending on the severity of the loss, the process of mourning may last for a long time, but eventually the grieving person begins to feel better and wants to move forward with her life.

For others, like Samantha and Tina, their loss quickly spirals into depression. What's the difference between the person who mourns her loss but knows that someday she will reenter life and the one who feels she doesn't want to or can't?

Jesus gives us a significant clue when he cautions us,

> Do not store up for yourselves treasures on earth, where moth and rust destroy, and where thieves break in and steal. But store up for yourselves treasures in heaven, where moth and rust do not destroy, and where thieves do not break in and steal. For where your treasure is, there your heart will be also (Matthew 6:19-21).

In this passage Jesus warns us of the reality of loss. Earthly things will be lost, stolen, broken, or destroyed. That's why he tells us not to center our heart in people or things. It's not that we can't enjoy them, or even want them, but when they are our primary focus or reason for living (Jesus calls them our "treasure"), the loss of those things creates an unbearable hole and life without them seems hopeless. This creates an environment for depression to flourish.

Samantha's treasure was in a Ph.D., her status as an "intellectual person," and what that dream brought to her self-esteem. When she lost it, she felt hopeless and worthless. Tina's treasure was her job and her reputation. Some women might consider their marriage or their physical appearance to be their treasure. Whatever captures our heart captures us. Jesus wants our treasure to be him and our hope to be in him. When we center ourselves in Christ alone, we're not shielded from sorrow or hardship, but we are protected from feelings of hopelessness when we face great losses in life.

Why Did Elijah Get Depressed?

Elijah was a godly man and one of Israel's most famous prophets. His story is told in 1 Kings 17–19. Elijah walked with God in total trust and obedience. He wasn't a spiritual slacker or a man of little faith. Elijah's word stopped the rain, and God used him to perform some of the Old Testament's most dramatic miracles. For example, he raised a child from the dead (1 Kings 17:21-22) and challenged the prophets of Baal to a showdown of strength in order to prove whose God was more powerful (1 Kings18:18-39).

After all his spiritual victory, why did Elijah suffer such a deep depression? There might be several ways to look at this, but most likely there were a number of factors at work. Sometimes there is great fatigue spiritually, emotionally, and physically after a mountaintop experience or spiritual success. Elijah certainly was exhausted. However, I don't think this fully explains his mental and emotional deterioration. To understand what happened to Elijah, it is important that we see not only what Elijah did, but who Elijah was and what he hoped for. In the whirlwind of his ministry and the miraculous things he did, Elijah's treasure began to subtly shift from hoping in God alone to hoping in what God would do next.

Elijah's deepest desire was to see Israel turn her heart back to God from her rebellion and idolatry. His sole purpose for the dramatic confrontation on Mount Carmel was to bring Israel to repentance. He longed to see King Ahab and the Jews know and trust God fully. Israel's initial response after witnessing fire fall from heaven might lead us to believe that Elijah got his wish, but it was merely intellectual agreement. God had Israel's attention, and she acknowledged that he was indeed more powerful than Baal. However, he still did not have Israel's heart or trust.

It's difficult to imagine why, after Elijah proved himself to be a true prophet of God, he would not be afforded the respect of the king of Israel. King Ahab witnessed God's supernatural power enabling Elijah to run ahead of his chariot to Jezreel, yet he did not invite Elijah to ride with him, nor did he repent. The king enjoyed the blessings of Elijah's prayer for rain but wanted nothing to do with Elijah's God. Instead, King Ahab told his wife, Queen Jezebel, everything Elijah did, and Jezebel, instead of repenting, ordered the prophet killed.

When Elijah heard this, his heart immediately was filled with fear and he ran once again, this time for his life. He grew despondent. "'I have had enough, LORD,' he said. 'Take my life; I am no better than my ancestors'" (1 Kings 19:4).

Elijah became depressed because he *lost* his treasure. He hoped that his life and ministry would have made a significant impact on Israel and that she would finally turn back to God. But as the ugly reality of Israel's stubborn heart sank deeply into the fiber of Elijah's being, depression loomed and he felt hopeless.

We too can become depressed when we hope in something other than God. Like Elijah, we can put our hope in good things, even godly, spiritual things. We hope for a restored marriage, a repentant prodigal child, or a meaningful ministry, but when it doesn't happen, we feel crushed and dismayed. We've lost our treasure, and our heart is broken. Satan loses no time in these moments, tempting us with doubts about God's goodness and sovereignty.

I love the way God tenderly cared for Elijah during his depression. He didn't scold or reject him. He recognized that Elijah's body was worn out and his perspective was distorted. God knew Elijah needed sleep and food, and the first thing God did was send an angel to care for Elijah's physical needs.

After Elijah was strengthened physically, God initiated a conversation. Elijah honestly told God how he felt (see 1 Kings 19:10) and God answered him. God showed him the reality of his presence and spoke to Elijah with grace and truth. God reminded Elijah there was more to the picture than he could see right now, and all was not lost.

Elijah believed he was the only one who was zealous for God, the only prophet left in Israel. The Lord gently corrected Elijah's misperceptions and false thinking. He reminded Elijah that he, God, was in control and had a plan. Elijah forgot those truths in the midst of his depression—and so do we.

Elijah's spiritual life would surpass most Christians' today, yet he still put all his hope in a good thing (Israel's repentance) instead of in the best thing (God alone). I am comforted by the verse in James where it reminds us that Elijah was a person, just like us (James 5:17).

What can we learn from Elijah's experience?

Listening to God

Something to Think About

When Elijah became depressed, he withdrew and isolated himself, yet God knew where he was and began to care for him. Elijah didn't resist the angel, nor did he argue with God when the Lord corrected his wrong thinking. Elijah didn't only talk with God and tell him his feelings; he listened to what God said back to him. Talking with God (prayer) is always a dialogue, not a one-way conversation.

Even when I'm not feeling blue, I find it difficult to listen to what God is saying to me. Sometimes I hear (or read) it, but the more strenuous part is to personally believe and trust it. I know I'm not alone.

As Jesus talked with Martha after Lazarus died, he must have noticed she was listening with her ears but not her heart. When he finished what he was telling her, he gently added, "Do you believe this?" (John 11:26). Often I hear Jesus asking me the same question. "Leslie, do you believe what I'm telling you?"

Jesus repeatedly says he is the truth and he is telling us the truth, but do we *really* believe him? Stop and ask yourself these questions:

- Would you feel different today if you really believed God loved you with his whole heart and deeply longed for you to love him back?

- Would you see yourself and your life more hopefully if you believed that he has a plan for your life that is good and for your good, even through this depression?

Everyone struggles with doubt and unbelief at times. Even the disciples doubted. When Jesus questioned the faith of a young father desperate for Jesus to heal his demon-possessed son, the man exclaimed, "I do believe; help me overcome my unbelief" (Mark 9:24).

The writer of Hebrews tells us that one of the reasons the Israelites did not feel God's comfort and peace was because of their unbelief (Hebrews 3:19). This happens to us when we say, "I know this in my head, but I don't feel it in my heart." The psalmist prayed, "Surely you desire truth in the inner parts; you teach me wisdom in the inmost place" (Psalm 51:6). At times many of us hear what God tells us with our intellect, but we don't take it as truth into our innermost being—our heart. This takes time and discipline.

Jesus says, "I have told you these things, so that in me you *may* have peace" (John 16:33, emphasis added). But he doesn't promise we *will* have peace. Why not? Because he knows that we will only experience a peaceful heart *if* we believe what he tells us is true.

Something to Do

In the last chapter we began to talk honestly with God about how we felt and all our problems. Now it's time to learn to hear him talking back to you. Connecting in a personal, heartfelt way to God is one of the most potent things you can do to feel hopeful when life is painful.

There are many different ways to listen to God. The most common is by reading small passages of Scripture and reflecting on them. Start by getting quiet. The Lord encourages us to "be still, and know that I am God" (Psalm 46:10). I start this process by sitting quietly with my eyes closed. I concentrate on my breathing, making it slow and deep. I start with four counts breathing in, 1...2...3...4, and four counts breathing out, 1...2...3...4. During those couple of minutes of quieting myself, I use my imagination to picture the cross or Jesus coming in and sitting in the chair next to me. I have my journal in my lap or on my desk with my pen. When my heart feels still, I begin to write out my feelings, my complaints, and my worries to God. I then read a portion of Scripture. It might be a whole chapter or maybe only a verse or two. I read until I feel there is something there for me.

Then I close my eyes again and ask Jesus to emphasize what he wants me to pay attention to that day. Is there something he wants me to know about himself? Something he wants me to change about myself? Something he wants me to think about differently? I write that down in red ink. Then I always picture him gently asking me, "Do you believe me?"

If you're at a loss as to where to read in your Bible, start with one of the Gospels: Matthew, Mark, Luke, or John. I like them because I can pay specific attention to the words that Jesus says. As you do this, remember to ask yourself, "Do I believe you, Lord?" Don't fake it. If your honest answer is no, write down what you think stands in the way. Then ask Jesus to help your unbelief. Remember, you can't *make* yourself believe, so don't beat yourself up if you struggle to believe. Even faith to believe is a gift from God. Jesus tells us that even the tiniest bit of faith, the size of a mustard seed, can do great things (Matthew 17:20).

When depression is moderate to severe, it often feels impossible to read and comprehend anything, and the Bible is no exception. One of my clients began listening to the Bible on CD on her drive to work. During the 15-minute ride she would listen and then afterward ask herself, "What are you saying to me today, Lord?" She would write down what she felt Jesus was telling her in her journal and conclude by asking herself the question, "Do I believe him?"

Others have told me that listening to music, especially praise and worship music, and lyrics that speak of God's faithfulness, grace, and love have lifted their spirits and helped them learn to trust him more. While the music is playing, listen quietly to what he is telling you about himself, about how life works, and about who you are to him. Write down what speaks to your innermost heart in your journal.

Remember, Elijah's experience with depression shows us that it can happen to anybody, even the most spiritually minded and mature person. Depression impacts one's body, mind, and emotions, and is often triggered by outside losses and stress.

Elijah's story reassures us that God cares about the depressed person and her suffering. God addressed Elijah's physical needs first, and when necessary, your physical symptoms must take first priority in dealing with depression. Without adequate sleep and proper nourishment for Elijah's body, God knew that Elijah's mind and emotions wouldn't be able to process what God had to tell him.

Depression often brings a woman to the edge of a cliff and then pushes her off. She can either fall into the pit of despair or fall into the presence of God's grace and love for her. Elijah fell into the arms of God and God held him tight—and he will hold you too.

My Body: Friend or Foe?

Be merciful to me, LORD, for I am faint;
O LORD, heal me, for my bones are in agony.
My soul is in anguish. How long, O LORD, how long?
PSALM 6:2-3

Learn to appreciate and give dignity to your body,
not abusing it, as is so common among those
who know nothing of God.
1 THESSALONIANS 4:4 MSG

One Sunday during a sermon my pastor asked the question, "When is a train most free to act like a train? When it is on the tracks or off the tracks?" Of course the answer is obvious: When it is on the tracks. When a train goes off the tracks, it is derailed and useless as a train. In fact, a train off the tracks can be quite dangerous and destructive.

When is a human being most free to be and act like a human being? Our world would like us to believe that we are most free when we are allowed to live as we please with no restraints. When we do that however, the Bible warns us that we will end up in bondage (2 Peter 2:19). God made us. It makes sense that we are most free to be who we were designed to be if we live our lives within the restraints our Maker intended. When we fall off his track, we get sick, hurt, or broken.

When Adam and Eve sinned, humankind fell off track. We live in an imperfect world where bad things happen to us and to those we love. We have imperfect bodies that break down and go haywire. We have imperfect hearts that are deceived, rebellious, stubborn, proud, foolish, broken, weak, and wounded. It's not hard to see why depression prevails.

God created human beings with a physical and spiritual dimension. Our body is what houses our spirit. Many women have a love/hate relationship with their body, and I'm not just referring to our American obsession with our physical attractiveness. We neglect our body and at the same time indulge it. We feed it the wrong things and fail to provide our body with things it needs to work best. Our body functions as our personal powerhouse and energy source that enables us to maneuver in this world. When our body is sick, it affects our inner life, and, conversely, we cannot disconnect our inner life from its effects upon our body.

Before we look at the question of whether antidepressant medication is the best choice to help the symptoms of depression, I want to help you understand the basic characteristics of our body, how it functions, and why it breaks down. Then we will look at how we need to care for our body as well as the issue of additional aids when our body is sick, especially the pros and cons of using antidepressant medications.

Characteristics of Our Body

The psalmist declares that "we are fearfully and wonderfully made" (Psalm 139:14). But we are not perfect anymore. Our body is subject to illness, decay, and death. Fortunately, our body also has some marvelous capabilities and mechanisms to heal, change, and grow.

Our Body Is Imperfect

There are things that go wrong in our body we have no control over. No matter how well we take care of ourselves or how spiritually mature we are, our body breaks down and gets sick. That is one of the inevitable consequences of the Fall.

There are certain diseases that cluster in families. Diabetes, coronary artery disease, high blood pressure, and certain forms of cancer are examples of the physical problems that particular individuals may be more biologically predisposed to through family genetics. Research among identical twins (those who share the same genes) shows that when one twin is depressed, the other twin is more likely to get depressed than if the twin was a fraternal twin (one who doesn't share the same genes). Heredity plays a role in depression. There is also strong evidence to support the theory that bipolar disorder has some genetic components.[1]

Pregnancy, childbirth, hormonal changes, menopause, and even stress can throw our body's chemistry out of balance, and depression may be the result. According to UCLA neuropsychiatrist Peter Whybrow, depression throws the basic housekeeping rhythms of the brain into disarray. He says,

> Sleeping and eating become disordered (along with libido), and energy levels dissipate, so that the simplest chore or social interaction can seem impossible. Further, the depressed brain fires off counterproductive distress signals of doom, gloom, fear, anxiety, panic, and self-destruction. Cognitive abilities like concentration and memory are sabotaged.[2]

Depression is also more likely with certain medical illnesses, such as multiple sclerosis, chronic fatigue, cancer, heart disease, diabetes, hormonal disorders, and Alzheimer's disease.

I've had one medical problem after another, starting with a hysterectomy, which really threw my emotions into turmoil.   *~ Pam*

I have been on medication (Zoloft) three times for about a year at a time after the birth of both boys and after my

*hysterectomy. It seems hormones really affect my moods
and depression. Currently, I am feeling better, but I still
struggle with depressed moods.*   ~*Janet*

In spite of our physical limitations, God can use our imperfect body to do important work. The apostle Paul was afflicted with a physical problem. We're not exactly sure what it was, but he called it a thorn in his flesh, and he said Satan used it to torment him. I wouldn't be surprised if Paul's thorn was depression, as he shares freely throughout 2 Corinthians about feeling discouraged and depressed at times (see, for example, 2 Corinthians 1:8-9 and 7:5-7). Paul pleaded with God to remove this thorn, but he didn't. Instead, God told Paul, "My gracious favor is all you need. My power works best in your weakness" (2 Corinthians 12:9 NLT).

Recently, one of my clients told me that although she'd prefer not to be depressed, she sees how God uses her to speak with others who also struggle with depression. This observation gave her joy even in the midst of her pain.

Our Body Is Self-Protective

Our body is designed with a wonderful self-protective mechanism to shield itself against harm. When something threatens our eyes, we automatically blink. When we get a tiny splinter, the rest of our body works to get it out. If something foreign is heading down our throat, we gag. Our hands and arms automatically shield our face if we're being attacked, and our immune system has its own internal army to fight germs and malignant substances.

One way of looking at depression is the body's attempt to protect itself. When depressed, our body starts to shut down and our mind and willpower become sluggish, even immobile. This may be our body's defense to protect itself from overwhelming stress and emotions that threaten our well-being. Unfortunately, once a body is deeply depressed, our mind usually cannot receive truth or help without some medical intervention.

Our Body Experiences Our Thoughts and Feelings

Our body is not independent of our inner life, and what we think and feel are experienced in our body. For example, when we feel afraid, our pulse quickens, and when we receive bad news, our heart aches. We get a sinking feeling in the pit of our stomach when we've realized we've forgotten to do something important or locked ourselves out of our car. Who hasn't felt the surge of physical power in the midst of their fury?

Paul described this duel distress when he wrote, "This body of ours had no rest, but we were harassed at every turn—conflicts on the outside, fears within" (2 Corinthians 7:5). Because of this interplay between our inner life and our body, it's hard to say which comes first when it comes to depression. The most honest answer is "It depends" or "It's hard to tell." That's why it is so important that we take a holistic approach to healing. Depression may start in the body and work its way inward, or start in our inner being and work its way out into our body. Either way, depression affects both body and spirit, and we must attend to both.

The need to pay attention to how our body affects our emotions is not a new idea that psychology has promoted. In a religious book written on depression in 1844, the author writes, "Cases often occur in which there is a mixture of moral and physical causes; and these should be treated in reference to both sources of their affliction. Melancholy is sometimes hereditary, and often constitutional."[3]

Our Body Has a Mind of Its Own

There are times that our body does something totally opposite from what we want it to do. For example, no matter what I do, I cannot stop my knees from trembling whenever I sing in public. My children won't attend a scary movie with me because I always scream (out loud) when I'm startled, even when I try not to and put my hand over my mouth. Some women have described waking up from a sound sleep in the grip of an anxiety attack with no recollection of any negative or anxious thoughts or dreams. Other women experience irritable bowels when anxious or upset, or sometimes for no apparent reason at all, and, therefore, never travel without knowing a bathroom is readily available. We become frustrated when our body acts up in ways we don't want it to.

Our body also has the ability to habituate itself to whatever we repetitively do. Athletes and musicians capitalize on this and train their body to respond correctly so that they don't have to consciously think anymore about what to do; their body remembers. This principle operates in all bodies, even those that are not athletically or musically inclined.

For example, most of us daily correspond with people by e-mail with our fingers doing the talking. We don't think about where to place our fingers on the computer keyboard or even where the alphabet is anymore; it's automatic. This is a good thing because it makes life much easier. Our body's ability to habituate quickly also results in some bad habits of responding or reacting that seem so normal that we don't stop to think about them anymore.

As athletes and musicians know, we can train our body to respond differently with time and concerted effort. When I wanted to stop biting my nails, my fingers still automatically went up to my mouth whenever I felt stress. Sometimes I'd bite my nail off before I realized what I was doing. To stop this ingrained automatic habit, I had to work to be more conscious of what my body was doing and train my body to develop new habits of coping with anxiety. Our body can be retrained. We can learn to handle our anxiety, anger, and stress in ways that don't cause our body to become ill or destructive to ourselves or to others.

Taking Care of Our Body

God masterfully created the human body, but it requires certain essentials for it to be healthy and thrive. When we ignore the basics of good self-care, we are more vulnerable to getting sick.

Our Body Needs Sleep

First, our body requires regular rest. For most of us that means at least eight hours of good sleep. We can go without food for a while, but we cannot function without adequate sleep. These days most of us ignore this important physical need. We foolishly think we can cheat our body of its rest and still perform at our best.

Margaret's depression improved after starting the antidepressant medication her doctor prescribed, but she was still not going to bed at a reasonable hour. Margaret stressed herself out over everything she needed to do to keep everyone—including herself—happy. Those tendencies were some of the things that led to Margaret's depression in the first place.

Although the medicine helped Margaret feel better, she continued to rob her body of sleep in order to get more done, rationalizing that she could get by on six hours of sleep instead of eight. Finally, her body rebelled. Driving home from a hectic day at work, Margaret fell fast asleep at the wheel and crashed into a parked car. Frightened, yet relieved she hadn't killed someone, Margaret finally accepted that her body needed more sleep and worked to change her evening routine. The two extra hours of sleep made a dramatic difference in Margaret's mood. "I feel so much better," she said. "I'm not as irritable and on edge as I was before. I thought I could get by on less sleep, but I was wrong. I need eight hours to function at my best."

Our Body Needs Good Food and Water

Our body also needs healthy and adequate nourishment and water. Although we might not die eating a steady diet of junk food, caffeine, and soda, those things take a toll on our health and mood. When I overindulge my chocolate cravings (which I am often tempted to do), I feel its affects upon my mood almost instantly. When I am sluggish (because I didn't get enough sleep), I tell myself that a candy bar or a couple of cookies, washed down with a Diet Coke, will get me over the hump and give me the boost of energy I need. And it does, temporarily, but then I pay the price. My sugar level drops back down and I'm irritable, down in the dumps, and anxious.

Today we hear a lot about the neurotransmitter serotonin, and how low serotonin levels are responsible for some depressions. Diana Schwarzbein, M.D., a leading authority on metabolic healing, says:

> Serotonin is one of the major neurotransmitters that affect mood. When serotonin levels are normal, mood is at its best. Normal serotonin levels provide a sense of well-being and contentment. Serotonin is the brain chemical that keeps your focus sharp and your concentration keen, enabling you to get a good night's sleep and to awake happy and energized. When your serotonin levels are normal, you are the most energetic and productive.[4]

In Dr. Schwarzbein's book, *The Schwarzbein Principle*, she advocates a natural way to raise serotonin levels in the brain through healthy eating habits, hormone replacements as needed, and nutritional supplements. She recommends "a diet sufficient in proteins, fats, non-starchy vegetables and natural carbohydrates." Dr. Schwarzbein says that our cravings for stimulants such as sugar, caffeine, tobacco, man-made carbohydrates, and alcohol stem from our low-serotonin state. These stimulants cause an immediate release of serotonin, which is quickly used up by the body. Then serotonin levels drop dramatically and you begin to feel down again. That explains why my candy bar and Diet Coke temporarily help my fatigue and sluggishness, but overall my mood actually gets worse. If we keep this habit up, she says, we can eventually deplete our natural storage of serotonin in our brain and end up depressed.[5]

If you struggle with mild depression, changing your diet may be sufficient to elevate the serotonin in your brain. Studies suggest a food intake in which 35 percent of your total daily nutrients come from lean protein, at least 25 percent from essential fats, and 40 percent from good carbohydrates. Whey protein, found in foods like turkey and reduced fat and fat-free dairy products, is especially helpful in providing tryptophan, an amino acid essential to creating serotonin. Good protein and omega-3 fats are found in wild salmon, black cod, and shellfish. Eggs, flaxseed, and unrefined oils also provide healthy sources of good fat. Adding low-to-moderate glycemic carbohydrates to your diet, such as whole grains, fruits, vegetables, nuts, and legumes, are helpful in stabilizing mood.[6]

For many reasons the majority of the woman I know struggle to eat well. One cause may simply be the multiple priorities we juggle. Many women rush home from work just in time to take their children to soccer practice or to music lessons. For them, after a long day at work, it's easier and less stressful to drive through the local fast-food restaurant than to plan for and prepare something nutritious.

Other women don't eat healthy meals because they are always trying to lose weight. They view their body as their enemy, thwarting their dreams for the good life or the perfect man. If only they could lose that cellulite, erase those frown lines, or shed those extra 10 or 20 pounds, then life would be good. They continually measure themselves against women with beautiful airbrushed skin and flawless bodies featured on the pages of women's magazines. Always falling short of the ideal, these women are constantly disappointed with themselves and deprive their body of the nutrients they need to feel better and to function optimally.

Our Body Needs Exercise

No one would dispute the need for physical exercise for a strong and healthy body. However, knowing what is good for us *and* doing it are two different matters.

It's hard to do what's good for us when we don't *feel* like it. It's even harder to do it when we feel like doing something else—like staying in bed.

My good friend Janet Holm McHenry, the author of *PrayerWalk*, shares how combining praying with walking for exercise helped her depression. She says,

[Before prayerwalking] sometimes sadness would simply envelop me for no reason. I cried in closets. I drove away to nowhere in tears. I sat on my bathroom floor in the middle of the night, trying to rock away a very real hurt in my chest...

She continues,

The miracle of my life is that three months after I began prayerwalking, my depression was gone, and it has not returned.[7]

Regular aerobic exercise, 30 minutes or more, at least three times a week, has been shown to be an effective natural treatment for depression. Vigorous exercise produces endorphins, which are the body's natural antidepressant. Studies have demonstrated that "regular physical exercise may not only heal an episode of depression, but also probably can help prevent one."[8] When comparing the effects of jogging with the antidepressant Zoloft, researches at Duke University found that both approaches worked equally well. However, at a one-year follow-up, "more than a third of the patients who had been treated with Zoloft had relapsed, whereas 92 percent of those who had followed the jogging program were still doing well."[9] Other exercises, such as Pilates, working out with weights, and stretching, can help reduce stress and build overall good health.

These studies as well as others consistently demonstrate that it is a good idea for those of us who are depression prone to begin and stick to an exercise program for our long-term health and well-being.

I take MUCH better care of myself now. Before I got depressed I exercised three times a week. Now I make sure I do something active every day. I eat much better, and I sleep more. (Though getting to sleep is still a depression symptom I battle. Music and Scripture are helping some.) The biggest plus, I think, has been the nutritional

supplements I am taking. As my body is healing, I believe
it is helping my heart and soul to heal too.   ~ Trish

Our Body Works Best When We Maintain a Routine or Schedule

Over the past several months, I've traveled to two different countries halfway across the world. My eating schedule was different, not only in what I ate but when I ate it. I never had time to exercise. I got constipated, and then diarrhea hit. As soon as I returned to my own bed, my own pillow, my normal routine, and food I was used to, things in my body started to quiet down. It is amazing how much our body craves structure, ritual, and routine, and it functions best when we provide those things.

While you're depressed, try to keep things as routine as possible. Get up and go to bed at your normal times. Try to take a daily walk, even if it is only for five minutes. Shower and get dressed as you normally have in the past. Eat small, nutritious meals at least three to five times a day, even if you're not hungry. These things will take more energy to accomplish when you're depressed, but they will keep you from feeling worse and will help your body remember how to regulate itself.

God Cares About Our Bodies

We've already seen how God tended to Elijah's body when he was depressed. Jesus shows deep concern for people's physical needs. Matthew tells us that Jesus had "compassion on them and healed their sick" (Matthew 14:14). In another story a large crowd gathered to hear Jesus' teaching, and after he was finished he invited them to stay for lunch. Jesus prayed and a boy's small lunch miraculously became a feast for thousands (Matthew 14:16-18).

Jesus tells a story about how we are to care for one another when someone is physically hurting. A wounded man lay critically injured on the side of the road, beaten and half dead. Many people hurried by, pretending not to notice. Jesus commended the Good Samaritan for his compassion for the injured man when he soothed his wounds with medicine, bandaged them, and then brought him to an inn for his continued care. Jesus teaches us to go and do likewise (Luke 10:30-37 NLT).

Depression can be disabling physically, mentally, emotionally, and spiritually. A lack of sleep, an inability to eat, muscle aches, headaches, a heavy heart, and a growing knot in the pit of your stomach make you feel as if you want to curl up in a ball and play dead or wish you were. Depending upon the severity of your symptoms, you may need more than healing words to bind up your wounds. Like the injured man, you may need medicine to soothe you and help your body stabilize. The Good Samaritan didn't talk to the man about his problem before he cared for his hurting body. Talking came later. Francois Fenelon, a seventeenth-century churchman and Christian mystic, writes,

> As for natural sadness which comes from melancholy, that only comes from the body. Thus medicines and regulation lessen it. It is true that it always returns, but it is not voluntary. When God gives it, we endure it in peace, as we do fever and other bodily ills.[10]

Additional Aids for Depression

Medication

There is evidence in nature and in Scripture that God is not opposed to the use of medicine, and he created some plants to be used specifically for medicinal purposes. The Bible refers to a special balm in Gilead that was used to heal wounds (Jeremiah 8:22; 46:11). Wine and myrrh were mixed together as a painkiller (Mark 15:23), and a poultice of figs was heated and applied to boils (Isaiah 38:21).

The right medicine can be extremely helpful when your physical, emotional, and mental state are deteriorating and you are losing your ability to function. If you can't sleep, if you can't think, if you feel confused or totally numb, if you can't get out of bed, if you can't comb your hair, if you can't make it to work, or if you can't stop crying, you need to see your medical doctor immediately. Psychiatrist Valerie Davis Raskin writes, "Sometimes loving, kind, supportive, insightful, incisive, pragmatic, spiritual, therapeutic words do not help, or not enough. Sometimes depression or anxiety is so severe, you can't even listen in the first place."[11]

As we have already learned, depression has many components, but when it results in difficulty in everyday functioning, a woman usually finds some initial relief through the right medicine. Although antidepressant medication doesn't cure depression, it can relieve some of the symptoms of depression, which can be a great start toward getting better. However, medication doesn't always work for some people, or it works for a while and later its effectiveness diminishes. This can become discouraging, and a good working relationship with your doctor and therapist can help mitigate these setbacks.

I am not opposed to the careful and controlled use of medication for depression, but I do see a growing trend that deeply concerns me. I see many women relying on antidepressants to feel better, but neglecting the internal and relational work they need to do if their depression isn't purely physical to actually get better. One woman I spoke with recently told me, "I've been on antidepressants for years. I'm afraid to stop taking them because they help me get up in the morning and to get to sleep at night. But I've never looked at why I got depressed in the first place and I don't want to. As long as I can keep going, that's all I want to do."

This is dangerous thinking and dangerous living. Outcome research has shown individual therapy to be as effective as medication and sometimes more so in helping a depressed person recover.[12]

So how do you decide whether you should take an antidepressant or not? First, don't believe that antidepressant medicine is the cure-all for your depression. It can be a temporary support to help you get stronger and rebalance your body chemistry, but it doesn't cure depression any more than crutches cure a broken leg (although crutches are often a good and necessary part of the healing process). Psychologist Michael Yapko says, "The 'disease model' of depression and the value of antidepressant medications have been exaggerated. Biology is only a part of the depression story, and antidepressant medications are only a part of a total solution."[13]

Yes, use medicine if you need it in the short term, but don't rely on it to fix everything. Psychiatrist Karl Benzio says, "The cure is skills—spiritual, psychological, emotional, and relational."[14] Listen to the different experiences of women who tried antidepressant medication:

> *I took antidepressants for several years. They helped me cope, but they didn't change my situation.*   *~Jean*

> *I have taken antidepressants for about six months, although the dose is considerably lower now. The medication was effective in preventing me from further decline while allowing me to utilize what I learned in counseling. As my personal growth in counseling occurred, I became less reliant on the medication.*
>   *~Donna*

> *Medication helped me to function better and maintain an even keel emotionally, but it did not solve the underlying problems. It helped me to take the emotional edge off my situation so that I could begin to talk openly about what was going on.*   *~Karen*

> *I was prescribed medication, and most of it made me feel dead to any emotions.*   *~Kim*

No medication is perfect, and sometimes it takes trial and error for your doctor to discern what medication or combination of medications will best help you. Keep in mind that many times people experience unpleasant side effects before the medicine has a chance to reach the therapeutic levels your body needs to feel a reduction in your depressive symptoms. Usually the side effects lessen the longer you take the medicine, but be sure to keep a record of how you are feeling and any side effects you experience. That way, when you go to your next medical appointment, you will be prepared to discuss with your doctor how this medication is working and what are your best options.

The four most common subgroups of antidepressant medications are selective serotonin-reuptake inhibitors (called SSRIs), serotonin and norepinephrine reuptake inhibitors (SNRIs), tricyclic antidepressants (TCAs), and monoamine oxidase inhibitors (MAOIs). They work on different parts of the brain, and your doctor will select one depending upon your particular depressive symptoms and your medical and family history.

Selective serotonin-reuptake inhibitors (SSRIs). These are the most commonly prescribed antidepressants. Luvox, Celexa, Paxil, Prozac, Lexapro, and Zoloft are the most commonly presribed SSRIs. They usually cause little or no weight gain, which is important to most women; however, sexual side effects (usually decreased libido, painful intercourse, or inability to have an orgasm) are more common. Other side effects of SSRIs include nausea and/or diarrhea, insomnia or decreased need for sleep, feeling jittery or sedated, vivid dreams or nightmares, and headaches. There are ways to mitigate these side effects, and if they bother you, talk with your doctor about them.

If you are taking SSRIs and have difficulty breathing, have swelling in your joints, have racing speech, impulsivity, or euphoria, or have heavy menstrual flow with bruising or nose bleeds, contact your doctor immediately.

SSRIs are the most expensive of the antidepressants. For those without insurance that may be a prohibitive factor. The SSRIs are often very effective in helping a woman feel better. However, some caution is warranted. Recent studies have shown that:

SSRIs often lead to intense anxiety, lethargy, and distress when medication is discontinued. There's increasing evidence of at least a psychological dependency on these medications, which leads to considerable discomfort when clients stop taking them. This, in turn, makes discontinuing these medications more difficult.[15]

Tricyclic antidepressants (TCAs). These were the first antidepressants and include Elavil, Norpramin, Sinequan, Anafranil, Pamelor, and Tofranil. Studies have shown them to be as effective in alleviating the symptoms of depression as the newer SSRIs.[16] Usually your doctor will start you on a low dose and gradually increase the amount until you are at the therapeutic level. Adjustments to the medication are done through blood testing.

For those with insomnia, the TCAs help you sleep. They are available in generic form, so they are also the most cost effective. However, due to some of the side effects (especially weight gain), TCAs are not usually the first choice for women. Additional common side effects include constipation, dryness (mouth, eyes, vagina), sleepiness (especially in the morning), dizziness, urinary retention, and feeling jittery.

Again, as with any antidepressant, if you experience itching or rashes, breathing problems, joint pain or swelling, racing speech, suicidal thoughts, palpitations and/or chest pains, or fainting, contact your doctor immediately. The TCAs are highly toxic when ingested in large quantities, making them a poor choice for depressed women with suicidal thoughts.

Serotonin and norepinephrine reuptake inhibitors (SNRIs). Effexor, Effexor XR, and Cymbalta are the most common SNRIs prescribed. Nausea, dry mouth, constipation, increased sweating, difficulty sleeping, and loss of appetite are the mild side effects of these drugs. As with any medication you take, read the information on adverse reactions included with your prescription. If you experience unusual side effects or find any of them intolerable, contact your physician. He or she can try a different medication that may be a better fit for you.

Monoamine oxidase inhibitors (MAOIs). These include Marplan, Nardil, and Parnate and may be effective for atypical depressions. However, these medications are best prescribed and administered under the supervision of a psychiatrist. The biggest downside is that they have strict dietary restrictions (for example, no beer, aged cheese, anchovies, caviar, smoked meats, products made with MSG or yeast products), and require close attention to the risks of negative interactions with other medications.

In addition to the classifications of antidepressant medications noted above, there are medications that work in different ways and may be more effective for some people. The most common are Wellbutrin and Wellbutrin SR.

Mood stabilizers such as lithium, Depakote, and Tegretol are used to treat bipolar depression, as well as augmenting antidepressants for treating unipolar depression. Other mood stabilizers include Topamax, Trileptal, Lamictal, Abilify, Risperdal, Zyprexa, Seroquel, and Gabitril. When depression is chronic, severe, or recurrent, consider making an appointment with a psychiatrist. Psychiatrists have the most experience using, choosing, and understanding the medications for depression and the other problems that often accompany depression, such as anxiety, addictions, eating disorders, and attention deficit disorder.

If your doctor prescribes antidepressants, you may start to feel better in as soon as two weeks. For others it may take eight to twelve weeks, depending on the dose and the illness.

If you've been taking medicine for a while, do not stop taking your medicine or adjust the dosage without medical supervision. Some medicines need to be weaned off of gradually to minimize side effects. Even when tapering off gradually, certain individuals have reported serious withdrawal symptoms. "Patients coming off anti depressants have suffered chills and fever, sweating, retching, muscle spasms and sensations that feel like electric shocks."[17]

Please understand that antidepressants are powerful medications with significant side effects for some individuals. As helpful as they can be for those suffering with depression, they should be used wisely and not seen as a long-term solution for most people.

Homeopathic Medicine

An alternative to antidepressant medication is finding a physician that specializes in homeopathic medicine. Homeopathic physicians work with the body's immune system. The physician prescribes remedies to stimulate your body to heal itself. Homeopaths believe that stress, whether it is emotional, physical, relational, mental, or environmental, may trigger symptoms that manifest themselves in our body according to our unique weaknesses and genetics. Symptoms are not considered to be the problem but are indications of the imbalance that has occurred due to stress.

Treatment involves an extensive interview with the patient (up to two hours for an initial consultation) to evaluate the sources of stress, the unique way stress is causing symptoms to appear in that person, and to determine whether the symptoms the patient is experiencing are acute or chronic. Remedies vary according to the person's unique symptom picture biology as well as on the origin and duration of the problem. The positive side of this approach is that after the initial consultation, the remedies are relatively inexpensive (usually under $20 a month) and have minimal or no side effects. The patient is considered cured, not just because the symptoms have disappeared, but because medication is no longer needed. The initial exam is costly, but if you make sure the homeopath is an M.D., it is usually covered under your medical insurance.

In this approach you actively partner with your doctor to discern root causes of your problem. Once the remedy is given, you should begin to feel some improvement within 30 to 60 days. If you see no change during that time, your homeopathic physician will give you a different remedy. Finding a qualified homeopathic physician is best done through word of mouth, but look for a medical doctor who is a Board Certified Diplomate in Homeopathic Therapy. To find out more information on homeopathic medicine or to locate a physician who specializes in this approach, see "Resources for Depression" on page 238.

Electroconvulsive Therapy (ECT)

Despite its scary sound, ECT has shown promise for severely depressed or suicidal individuals who need immediate symptom relief, as well as people who have not obtained positive results from antidepressants or other treatments. A physician administers ECT under anesthesia and a small electrical charge is applied to one side of the brain. There is no memory of the procedure and often the person goes home the same day. The ECT treatment is repeated between eight and twelve times over a three-week period to hopefully achieve complete remission of the depressive symptoms.[18] The biggest drawback for most people is the negative connotations to ECT from past misuses and the temporary loss of some short-term memory.

Herbs, Nutritional Supplements, and Other Therapies

It is beyond the scope of this chapter to adequately cover the pros and cons of these alternative approaches. In their book A Woman's Guide to Overcoming Depression, Dr. Archibald Hart and his daughter Dr. Catherine Hart Weber have an excellent chapter on natural complementary treatments for depression. They encourage women to be cautious and research evidence for the effectiveness of such treatments, as well as to understand that taking herbal medicines for depression may interfere with other medicines they are taking or result in their own side effects. Yet, for mild to moderate depression, herbal antidepressants like Saint-John's-wort and complementary medicines, nutritional supplements, light therapy, and music therapy, as well as learning progressive muscle relaxation, can provide some relief and be good alternatives to antidepressant medication.[19]

Making Your Health a Priority

Something to Think About

In 1 Thessalonians 5:14 the apostle Paul encourages Christians to "warn those who are idle, encourage the timid, help the weak, be patient with everyone." The word "weak" in the original language does not refer to moral weakness but physical weaknesses or being sickly or infirm. Your body plays a significant role in depression. You may have a biological or genetic predisposition that makes you more susceptible to getting depressed than people who do not have this physical condition.

If you experience depression, stop blaming yourself for your physical limitations and/or weaknesses. None of us have perfect bodies. Some of us have vulnerabilities to allergies, some to cancer, others to obesity, diabetes, or high blood pressure. All the more reason we should take good care of our body and learn to deal with stress and relationship difficulties so that we minimize our risks of developing clinical depression or other illnesses. Notice that the apostle Paul doesn't scold people for their physical limitations; instead, he encourages the rest of us to help them and to be patient with them.

Something to Do

Pick one thing that was mentioned in this chapter that is necessary in caring for your body. It might be to start a walking program or enlist a friend to walk with you. Try adding more vegetables and fruits to your diet or eliminating sugar. Work on one thing for a month (you won't work on it perfectly, but practice it more than not), and notice if you see an improvement in your overall mood. If you are currently on antidepressants, I hope your goal is eventually to taper off of them. Therefore, you must learn to take better care of your body and provide it with what it needs in order to function well and lessen your vulnerability to future depressions.

In this chapter we have seen how problems in our body affect our inner life. Next, let's turn our attention to our inner life and how our thoughts and feelings impact our body and contribute to depression.

Understanding Myself

My back is filled with searing pain;
there is no health in my body.
I am feeble and utterly crushed;
I groan in anguish of heart.
PSALM 38:7-8

As water reflects a face,
so a man's heart reflects the man.
PROVERBS 27:19

A heart at peace gives life to the body.
PROVERBS 14:30

I'm so much better, Leslie," Mary announced during one of our counseling sessions. "I'm feeling like my old self again."

Remember Mary? When we first met her in chapter 1, she had a blotchy face, was embarrassed by her tears, and was scared of going crazy. Mary took the antidepressant medicine her doctor prescribed and also faithfully continued her counseling. Over the weeks and months Mary and I worked together, she realized she hated disappointing anyone or making a fuss. Mary always did what others wanted or didn't want her to do, even when it hurt her to do so—anything to avoid conflict. In her relationships Mary assumed the role of the strong one, the problem solver, the giver, and the caretaker. She rarely asked her family members or friends to help her, support her, listen to her, or care for her and meet her needs. On rare occasions when she did ask for help, they didn't respond positively. Mary often felt lonely, unloved, taken advantage of, and invisible as a person. She concluded she must be unworthy of love or attention.

Whenever Mary became angry or resentful about these things, she felt guilty. Afraid to rock the boat, she tried to keep her feelings to herself, stuffing them inside and denying them until she no longer felt anything but numb and scared. During our counseling Mary and I discussed her ways of caring for herself, relating to people, and handling life's problems. She realized that prior to her current depression, guilt and fear were feelings that ruled her life. Mary usually handled problems by avoiding them or ignoring them, pretending to others, and sometimes even to herself, that all was well.

But what Mary said next nearly took my breath away. Her depth of insight amazed me. She said,

> But, even though I'm feeling like my old self again, my old self got depressed. My old self doesn't know how to express my feelings or deal with conflict or ask for something back from others. My old self doesn't know how to connect with God the way I'd like to or have mutually satisfying relationships or set boundaries with people. My old self still tends to feel angry and fearful and guilty about everything. I struggle with the lies I've believed about myself, like I'm worthless, and I want to live more consistently believing God's truth. Feeling like my old self isn't good enough anymore. I want to get *better* than my old self.

Wow! Mary didn't want to just *feel* better anymore. She understood that to get better and become healthier, she needed to look at herself and evaluate her ways of thinking, feeling, and responding. As she did this, she saw what she needed to change so that she would mature and grow into the woman God designed her to be.

Depression is not only a physical condition. It is not just something that happens to us. Mary began to understand that she had a part in getting depressed. This is not to cast blame or to say it is her fault. Depression has many factors. However, in order to lessen Mary's vulnerability to future depressions, it is important that she identify the internal themes that made depression possible, such as perfectionism, false guilt, unresolved anger, wrong thinking, anxiety, and self-hatred. In addition to looking at these things, Mary learned to recognize and name the recurrent patterns of behavior that she used to cope with these feelings, such as avoiding conflict, people pleasing, and disconnecting from herself, others, and God. She also practiced different ways of looking at and handling her emotions so that they would not dominate her life as they had in the past.

Our physical body is one critical aspect of depression. Difficult life circumstances are another. What is going on inside of us (the Bible calls this our heart) is another important dimension to understanding both the causes and the way out of depression. Charles Spurgeon said, "A troubled heart makes that which is bad worse. It magnifies, aggravates, caricatures, and misrepresents. If just an ordinary foe is in your way, a troubled heart makes him swell into a giant."[1]

Mapping the Terrain of Our Heart

I get lost easily. Some call it being directionally challenged. Growing up, one of the most valuable skills I learned was how to read a map. Map reading is not something I do for fun; I do it when I'm lost or as a preventive measure to ensure I won't get lost and waste time when I'm traveling to a new place. Besides knowing where it is you want to go, one of the most important parts of map reading is to know how to locate where you are so that you can see how to get where you want to go.

Depression feels a lot like being lost in a dark cave with no light, no compass, no map, and no bread crumbs left to remind you of how you got there. It's terrifying. No one wants to wander around, hoping to stumble upon the way out. Although map reading may not be the most interesting thing to learn, it sure comes in handy and can save your life when you're lost in a scary place.

The best map and compass I know to show the way out of despair and into healthy living is God's Word. The Bible not only explains where we are now, but also how to get to where we'd like to be. And it warns us about the pitfalls to avoid along the way.

The Bible has much to say about the inner workings of our heart as well as how to have good relationships. These things are true for all people, not only depressed women. Knowing how God designed us gives us the ability to recognize what's gone wrong and how we got where we are. In his Word he provides us with tools we can use to find our way out of depression as well as other problems of life. Just as with maps and compasses, however, these tools only work if you learn to use them properly and apply them to your life.

The Bible clearly teaches that we have been created with a physical body and also with a soul, or spirit. I used to think God made human beings in three parts, with a body, soul, and spirit, but along with some scholars today I believe God created humankind as a two-part being: physical and spiritual.[2] The spiritual, inner part is who we are, our essence; in other words, our selfhood. The Bible refers to our nonphysical side from many angles, sometimes referring to it as our soul, sometimes as our spirit, and many times simply calling our inner self our "heart."

Contrary to Hallmark and other promoters of Valentine's Day, our heart does not only involve our emotions. Our heart is our essence, who we really are, and encompasses our personality, our desires, our thoughts and feelings, and what we cherish and value. Study notes in the New International Version of the Bible define our heart as "the center of the human spirit, from which spring emotions, thought, motivations, courage and action."[3]

The Bible tells us that our heart is "the wellspring of life," and that we should protect it vigilantly (Proverbs 4:23). There are many Scriptures that speak about the condition of a person's heart. Our heart can be divided, unruly, darkened, undisciplined, foolish, lying, deceived, broken, faint, hard, rebellious, stubborn, loving, kind, blameless, simple, or pure. Although our heart functions as a whole, it has different components. To understand how we become vulnerable to depression, let's look more closely at three main areas of our heart.

Components of the Heart

Our Feelings

Feelings are a lot like taste buds, both wonderful and terrible. I wouldn't want to be without them. They make the necessity of eating pleasurable, and when you've bitten into something foul, they warn you—spit it out now!

Our feelings contain our bodily sensations as well as our emotions. Emotions take us to the highest highs and the lowest lows of being human. Feelings can change in an instant. One moment we can feel happy, contented, and thrilled, and the next we are perplexed, sad, anxious, angry, guilty, or overwhelmed. Sometimes it's hard to put our deepest emotions into words, but our body always feels them. Our stomach turns, our head throbs, our muscles tighten, and our heart aches.

Negative feelings remind me of little children; they often demand our attention, and when we try to ignore them, they usually get louder and more disruptive. Most of us wish we felt only the more positive range of emotions, but negative feelings can also be informative. Like our taste buds, they often warn us that something is wrong so that we can take appropriate action.

Many depressed women have not learned to recognize certain feelings, especially anger. Instead, they usually deny their feelings or ignore them for as long as they can. They tell themselves it's easier to do so, but often what looks easiest is, in the long run, the more difficult path. Like Mary, instead of acknowledging their anger and figuring out what to do with it, depressed women usually deny it or stuff it back down, pretending to others and even to themselves that they don't feel what they feel.

> *During depression I checked out emotionally, merely going through the motions. I still struggle with falling into that easy default habit.*   ~ Gina

> *Depression is a place of escape for me. It allows me to justify inactivity toward resolving difficulties. It can also serve as protection against further loss of hope. Sometimes the familiarity of depression is preferable to the unknown consequences of working through issues and conflict to resolution. Depression can blunt intense feelings of pain. Sometimes that seems more comfortable than allowing myself to experience the pain.*   ~ Gwen

One day while cleaning, Judy stumbled upon a large collection of pornographic videos hidden in her husband's closet. Instead of feeling angry, which would be a normal reaction, Judy plummeted into depression. She carefully put them all back and pretended she hadn't seen them. It was easier for Judy to "forget" because if she felt her rage, she'd also have to face the possibility that her marriage was in deep trouble, and that possibility scared her to death.

There are other women who neither deny nor hide from their emotions but rather allow them to run rampant and unchecked by truth or reality. Anxiety, anger, and guilt are often the predominant emotions that control their heart. Although capable in many ways, these women quickly become overwhelmed by fear of failure and of never being good enough. They disdain their own imperfections as well as the flaws they observe in others. They often feel furious toward those who have hurt them and at the same time feel tremendous guilt for feeling angry. Their emotions paralyze them. They are unable to think or take appropriate action to help themselves or handle their problems in a godly way.

*I know that anger and depression are closely related some-
how. On the one hand, I get furious and rage when things
do not go right (my way), and on the other hand I go into
the helplessness and hopelessness of depression. Giving up
my "rights" to God, while at the same time looking for
healthy solutions to conflict, seems to help.   ~ Rebecca*

God created us with emotions, and he called his creation good. But
as with other good things God made, our emotions can be misused
and used for wrong purposes. God designed our feelings to inform us,
not control us. Feelings become cruel taskmasters when we let them
run our lives. For all of us, it is crucial that we learn how to control our
emotions rather than to allow our emotions to control us. Some of the
exercises at the end of the chapters will give you help in practicing this
important skill. Also, chapters 8 and 9 will show you ways to handle
the most common relationship difficulties so that you can handle your
emotions and situations in a constructive and godly way.

Your feelings are important, but they aren't always a reflection
of reality or truth. For example, like every other woman I know, sometimes I *feel* fat and ugly. I don't know why we get those awful feelings, but if I allowed them to control me, I would end up having a
miserable, horrible day. When I say the wrong thing, I often feel
stupid, but I know I'm not stupid. When we allow feelings of shame
and inferiority or physical unattractiveness to consume us with self-
pity or self-hatred, we not only feel miserable for the moment, but
often much longer.

Right now in your depression you may feel fearful, angry, guilty,
sad, hurt, worthless, abandoned, or hopeless. Understand that feelings are not just free-floating emotions that happen to us. It's true
they are often triggered by external circumstances, such as loss, but
emotions always go through the filter of our own interpretive lens.
God hardwired our feelings to our thoughts. When we struggle with
negative feelings about ourselves, others, or life, the next question
we must ask ourselves is, what are we telling ourselves? Our feelings

are connected to our thoughts and deepest beliefs, and these are what make up the second dimension of our heart.

Our Thoughts and Beliefs

Human beings are thinking creatures. God gave us the ability to reason, imagine, and create. We continuously interpret what's happening to us through the thoughts we think. Whether you want to admit it or not, you talk to yourself. Everyone does. That is how we make sense of our feelings, bodily sensations, and the world around us. For example, this morning I woke up with pain in my chest and arms. I told myself my new exercise routine must be working some new muscles. I felt pleased as I pictured my arm flab disappearing and then jumped out of bed, ready to start my day.

But I would have felt and responded differently had I interpreted my chest pain with the thought, *I must be having a heart attack!* Instead of feeling happy, I would have felt terrified, and rather than getting ready for work as usual, I would have been dialing 9-1-1.

How we think and *what* we think about directly affects our emotions and, to a great extent, our body and our behavior. The psalmist cried out, "My thoughts trouble me and I am distraught" (Psalm 55:2). Most people don't understand this important principle. They either see their emotions and moods as feelings that descend upon them out of the blue, or they believe that their emotions are caused by unpleasant or difficult situations. But this is not true. "Feelings are not independent parts of the human psyche that fire off at will unless there is a biological breakdown. Emotions are linked to the thoughts that we have about ourselves and the people in our world."[4] How I interpreted or "thought" about my chest pain is what gave me the emotions I felt. In this particular example, I did have some evidence to support my initial thought that they were due to my exercises, but I could have been wrong.

Situation	Thoughts	Feelings	Behavior
Morning chest pain	Good, my exercises are working.	Happy	Started my morning routine

Situation	Thoughts	Feelings	Behavior
Morning chest pain	I must be having a heart attack.	Fear, panic	Called 9-1-1

Remember when we looked at Elijah's depression in chapter 2? Elijah became depressed because he lost his hope that Israel would repent. But let's listen in on what he was telling himself about the situation (1 Kings 19).

Situation	Thoughts	Feelings	Behavior
Elijah flees Ahab and Jezebel	I have had enough, Lord. I am no better than my ancestors. I have been very zealous for you, Lord. The Israelites have rejected your covenant, broken down your altars, and put your prophets to death with the sword. I am the only one left, and now they are trying to kill me too.	Hopelessness, despair	Slept, withdrew

We can see that some of what Elijah was telling himself was true, but some of it was not. It was true that Israel didn't fully repent, but it wasn't true that his ministry was a waste or that he was the only prophet left. Yet because he thought those things, Elijah felt discouraged and hopeless. God gently corrected Elijah's thinking when he told Elijah that he was not the only one left and that God still had a plan for Israel (see verses 15-18).

You will recall that God first addressed Elijah's depression by personally caring for his body. After Elijah was physically rested and renewed, God spoke truth to Elijah's heart (corrected his thinking).

God still longs to show us how to see things from his perspective so that our emotions and our body will feel his peace and joy, even in the most difficult situations (Isaiah 26:3; James 1:2-4). The psalmist knew this important principle. He said,

> I will praise the LORD, who counsels me; even at night my heart instructs me. I have set the LORD always before me. Because he is at my right hand, I will not be shaken. *Therefore my heart is glad and my tongue rejoices; my body also will rest secure* (Psalm 16:7-9, emphasis added).

When a woman is depressed, those negative and hopeless feelings not only affect her body, but they also influence her thoughts. She sees things through a negative lens that distorts what is true. For example, when she makes a mistake, she tells herself she's stupid and can't do anything right. If her boyfriend or husband rejects her, she tells herself that she's unlovable, unattractive, or worthless.

A healthy individual knows at least at some level that these thoughts or statements are not true, but for the depressed person they *feel* true. Our emotions don't distinguish whether we are thinking truthfully or not. Thoughts of suicide and death are common for people who are depressed. Psychologist Michael Yapko writes,

> I have come to believe that the chief problem with most depressed people is that they think, feel, and act out of a depressive perspective that is distorted and hurtful, and then make the mistake of actually believing this perspective is a God-given truth.[5]

Donna learned this, and so did Veda and Janet. For you to get better, you must begin to recognize the connection between what you tell yourself (your thoughts) and how you feel.

> *The most helpful thing I learned in counseling is recognizing that depressed people think negative thoughts. I am typically an optimist, and I didn't even realize I was*

thinking so negatively. Now that I know about these neg-
ative thoughts, I am more aware of them and have ways
in which to deal with them. In particular, I have to think
about the truthfulness of these negative thoughts and force
myself to shift my thinking so that I look at things dif-
ferently. Consciously thinking about the negative thoughts
has made a difference in the way I handle situations.

~ Donna

I'm typically a happy and contented person; when I was
depressed I had extreme thoughts of things being wrong.

~ Veda

I realized that my mindset had a lot to do with my
depression.   *~ Janet*

Some women who aren't clinically depressed still may think negatively about things. Their pessimism is usually due to personality
types as well as upbringing. This style of thinking makes women more
prone to becoming depressed when they experience loss or stress in
their lives. Habitually thinking negatively also causes someone to feel
more unhappy and dissatisfied, and have greater emotional distress
than the person who tends to think more positively. Likewise, the
woman who is able to check her negative thoughts until she has more
evidence to support the truth of them will have a greater ability to
fight against negative feelings associated with unverified negative
thoughts.

Although I wasn't depressed at the time, here's an example of how
my negative thoughts affected my emotions, my body, and my
behavior. One evening my 17-year-old daughter was out with her
friends. It started snowing heavily. I became anxious. Was this anxiety because it was snowing? Not exactly. I felt anxious because of what
I was thinking. Once again let me show you how this works:

Situation	Thoughts	Feelings	Behavior
Daughter out, started snowing	What if they get into an accident? They don't know how to drive in snow.	Anxiety fear	Pacing, looking out window
	Why doesn't she call me?	Anger	Trying to call her cell phone

If I think anxious thoughts, I feel anxious. If I start to feel anxious and think negative thoughts, I will become more anxious and upset. When we habitually think negative thoughts about ourselves, we usually feel guilty about everything, have no self-esteem, and may even hate ourselves. An unhealthy thought life will ruin us. Whether we allow our mind to dwell in perversions or worry or chronic negativity, we are mapping out our character by the habits of our imagination.

> *I am my own worst enemy. I am very critical, unforgiving, and negative. There is no other person I have ever been so hard on.*   *~Edie*

Our thought life *always* affects our emotions and our body in some way. When I am watching a scary movie, I feel scared and become tense as adrenaline starts preparing my body for fight or flight. The only thing that keeps me from panic is the thought that this is not really happening, it's just a movie. That's why people enjoy those kinds of movies. They can get the rush of scared feelings in a controlled environment (without actually living through the real experience).

In order to effectively fight depression, I am not saying we must replace all of our negative thoughts with positive ones. Eliminating negative thoughts, especially when they reflect reality and truth, is not a healthy way to live. For example, if I am having chest pain and

I only tell myself positive thoughts, I may die. God doesn't teach us to think positively about life, but he does tell us to think truthfully (Philippians 4:8) and to take every thought captive to the obedience of Christ (2 Corinthians 10:5).

Getting over depression doesn't mean we always feel happy or think great and wonderful thoughts. But it does mean that we are starting to figure out how to deal with the difficulties in our life and face them with God's help instead of living in fear, running away, pretending everything is fine, or allowing negative feelings to rule and potentially ruin our life. If you are currently depressed, challenging your thoughts may be difficult to do alone. You may make more progress with the help of a Christian counselor.

> *I was given a different perspective on several situations, and that helped me. I realized that some of my perspectives were unhealthy and not based in reality or in God's ways or Word like I thought they were.*   ~Cindy

> *The ability to think deeply is a gift, but at the same time it is my greatest weakness. I cannot save myself from depression by relying on "thinking" my way out apart from God. I need to listen to him and let his words and his presence direct my thinking.*   ~Gwen

Our heart alone cannot always discern the things that are true, good, or right. But Jesus promises us that he gives us a personal Counselor, the Spirit of truth, who will guide us into all truth (John 15:26; 16:13). Being willing to listen, willing to learn, willing to grow, and willing to apply what we learn takes us to the last component of our heart—our will.

Our Will

Our will is extremely important. When our will is under the control of God's truth, it can help us overrule our temporary mood and challenge untrue thoughts with the truth. How our will consistently chooses to handle our inner life, our relationships, and the circumstances beyond our control is what makes us uniquely who we are. While imprisoned in the concentration camps during World War II, Viktor Frankl observed the power of choice. He said,

> We who lived in concentration camps can remember the men who walked through the huts comforting others, giving away their last piece of bread. They may have been few in number, but they offer sufficient proof that everything can be taken from a man but one thing: the last of the human freedoms—to choose one's attitude in any given set of circumstances, to choose one's own way.[6]

The most important questions God asks us have to do with our will. Are we willing to believe that his truth and that his way are the only way to find life? Are we willing to trust and obey him? Or like Eve, do we want to go our own way and trust our own thoughts and emotions? The first woman was deceived through her thoughts, and then she made a poor choice based on her emotions. Satan tempted her with the thought that God wasn't looking out for her good when the Lord forbade her from eating the fruit of the tree of knowledge. As she allowed that thought to take root in her heart, she began to feel cheated, and her desire for the forbidden fruit grew.

Instead of choosing to believe what God said, Eve acted upon her own thoughts and feelings and ate the fruit. At one time she knew the truth, but chose (her will) to disregard it because she came to believe a lie more than the truth.

Due to the Fall, everyone's will as well as their thoughts and emotions are naturally bent toward going their own way instead of trusting God. For the seriously depressed woman, this temptation can be fatal. It may look like this. Evelyn feels hopeless. Her depression becomes unrelenting emotional pain and her body can't function. She sleeps all the time or she can't sleep at all. She can't concentrate on anything. She knows that suicide is wrong and not God's will for her life, yet she is tempted with some alluring thoughts that feel true but in reality are lies. "It will soon be over. I'll be at peace. It's a way to get rid of my pain. No one cares anyway. God doesn't love me. My children will be better off without me. I can't take it anymore." Evelyn makes an emotional decision based on lies because she is unwilling or unable at that moment to believe what God says over her own subjective thoughts and feelings. Her will is captive to her feelings and thoughts. As with Eve, the consequences of Evelyn's decision are forever and life changing, not only for Evelyn herself, but for everyone who knows and loves her.

In his excellent book *Renovations of the Heart,* Dallas Willard writes:

> The "CEO" of the self [the will] has abandoned its post to other dimensions of the self and is dragged hither and thither by them. In our culture today the direction of the self is usually left to the feelings; and the will, if it is recognized at all, is either identified with feelings or else regarded as helpless in the face of feelings.[7]

It is part of being human to struggle with a divided heart and even with a divided will. We want to trust God *and* we want to trust our own ability to go our own way. God says that he works with us to strengthen our will so that we will be able to make good and right choices in life even when we have emotions and thoughts that are in conflict with our deeper desires (Philippians 2:13). Wanting what God wants and a desire to be made willing are important parts of becoming more like Christ, even in the midst of great suffering.

Yet willpower alone is never strong enough to permanently change our behavior. Our will may coax us toward what we believe is the right path, but it is never sufficient to keep us there if the rest of our heart and our body are unwilling. However, as we learn to guard and discipline our whole heart, healthier emotions and true thoughts, as well as our will, can work together to help us choose right actions when our depressed moods or negative thoughts tempt us to despair and to give up.

> *I've learned that our mind plays tricks on us and that if I want to be healed from depression, it's possible but will take work on my part. I also found that what I believed was not working at the time ended up to be the very thing that saved me.*   ~Audrey

Habits of the Heart

As human beings, repetitive motions of our inner self, over time, become ingrained into the interior fiber of our being. As with our body, our heart develops patterns of thinking, feeling, and responding or not responding. These form our inner attitudes, our deepest motivations and habits of being, which we define as our character—whether it be good or bad. These things become so automatic that we don't consciously think of them anymore. They are just "the way we are."

To change "the way we are," we need to recognize the automatic ways of our heart and allow God to transform them into his ways. The apostle Paul speaks of this process when he says,

> You were taught, with regard to your former *way of life,* to put off your old self, which is being corrupted by its deceitful desires; to be *made new in the attitude of your minds;* and to put on the new self, created to be like God in true righteousness and holiness (Ephesians 4:22-24, emphasis added).

In this passage Paul is speaking of changing our feelings, our thinking, and our behavior as we respond to God's truth with a willing heart that wants to surrender to his ways. This process always begins in our mind, but it isn't achieved merely by learning new information. The truth we need isn't informational truth, but transformational truth. Truth isn't something we learn, it is Someone we know. Jesus tells us that he is the truth (John 14:6).

Lasting change happens when we experience God in a new way. We see him differently. We start to see God as for us and not against us (Romans 8:31), and that reality brings hope to the hopeless heart. We believe him to be good and only desiring our good, and that truth brings peace to the heart that is full of fear (Romans 8:28-29). Our thoughts and feelings toward God motivate our will to surrender and obey, not because we have to, but because we want to. He tells us to trust him with all of our heart (our emotions, our mind, and our will), and not to lean on our own understanding (Proverbs 3:5-6).

In Jerusalem, Jesus met a man who had been paralyzed a long time. He asked him a puzzling question: "Do you want to get well?" (John 5:6). Why would he ask that? Sometimes we become so used to the way we are, it's hard and it's scary to change and live differently. Jesus told this man what he would need to do in order to get well (verse 8). Are you willing?

Learning
Self-Control

Something to Think About

The Scriptures provide a dramatic account of God bringing life to something that was dead. The bones of skeletal corpses gained some flesh, but were still corpses until God breathed his life into them (Ezekiel 37). God can put flesh on your dry bones and new breath in your deadened soul. He calls you to come forth, to walk in newness of life. Jesus asks you, "Do you want to be healed?"

This book is not about formulas to get rid of depression or even for living the Christian life. I want you to know God better and to see yourself the way he sees you, but you must be willing. Being willing is the first step, but it is not the last. We may want to do many things, such as lose weight, save money, run a marathon, or become healthier, but if we don't learn *how* to do these things and *practice* doing them, we will not achieve the things we want to do. God's Word tells us to apply what God is showing us to our daily life (Proverbs 23:12).

This is where self-control and self-discipline come in. Without these skills, life becomes a mess. This happens with our physical bodies and our inner life as well as with our relationships with others. For example, when we fail to control our eating, we gain weight or become sick. If we recklessly wound others with a tongue that is out of control, we hurt others and ruin relationships. Learning self-control over my body means I choose (my will) to do physical exercise because it is consistent with wanting to be healthy and in reasonably good shape (my thoughts/beliefs/desires). Rarely do I feel like it (temporary feelings). I want to be healthy (my thoughts, feelings, and will are involved with this desire), but I always feel like eating junk food, especially chocolate (bodily cravings due to ingrained bad habits). I choose (my will, exercising self-control) not to give in to my temporary emotional state or fleshly appetites (most of the time) because they are inconsistent with the person I want to be and become. The benefit is that as I become healthier and stronger physically, I feel better and like myself more. The Bible warns us that the consequences of an undisciplined life is self-hatred (Proverbs 15:32).

Learning to deny ourselves what we want isn't meant to make us more miserable. It is always a means to gain something better. No one gets to have it all. Therefore, we often must be willing to give up something we like for something we want. For example, I choose to give up eating everything I want in order to stay at a reasonable weight. I let go of my tendency toward self-pity in order to take responsibility for my life and become mentally and emotionally stronger. To have a happy marriage, I need to give up my selfish ways. Jesus tells us that when we are willing to give up our lives for him, we end up finding our life (Matthew 10:39).

The miracle that occurs when I deny myself these small things is that I gain so much more. I gain more health, more love, more virtue, more purpose to my life, more depth of character, more self-respect, more self-control and discipline, and greater self-esteem. Not a bad trade.

Understand this crucial truth. We are always in the process of becoming. We are either becoming better or worse, healthier or not, more godly or more sinful, more willing or more willful. We get to choose which direction we will walk in.

Something to Do

As we have already learned, God designed our emotions to inform us, not control us. When we are depressed, our emotions become dictators. Our emotions are not the only part of who we are. We have other parts of ourselves to draw from. For example, I never feel like getting out of bed (my emotions). There is even a small part of my thoughts that collude with these feelings by telling myself, *Just one more minute, one more minute.* But then my will kicks in and says, *Get up now* and my thoughts join in and tell myself, *If you don't, you're going to be late,* and so my body complies. Once I'm in the shower, I start feeling better. We not only can draw on other parts of ourself when we don't feel like changing something, but we also have a heavenly Father who wants us to turn to him when our heart is faint.

Close your eyes and use your mind to imagine your emotions handing the reins of control over to God. Your will is consenting to this transfer of power. Your emotions must now learn to find their proper place in your life. They will be under the authority of God's truth. Each time your emotions grab the reins back, exercise your will (your choice), to surrender them back over to God. As you practice this, your emotional life will find greater stability and unity. Thomas Kelly says, "The crux of religious living lies in the will, not in transient and variable states."[8]

After this exercise, go back over your journal of talking with God about your feelings and his responses. Look for your own thoughts and notice how they are linked to what you are feeling. Observe whether you allowed what God had to say to you from previous journal entries to penetrate your heart. Whose words spoke louder—your own thoughts and feelings or God's Word? Who gets the final say? Read James 1:22 and write it in your journal. Are you willing to allow God's Word to heal and transform your heart?

Lonely Heart

She put her heart into a box
And placed it on the shelf.
She thought it would be easier
To hide it from herself.

As life demanded much from her
And days turned into years
She saw the love that she once knew
Slowly disappear.

She learned to live her life this way
Behind a well-built mask
Ignoring pain and emptiness
Completing every task.

The heart was growing lonelier.
It sat collecting dust.
It watched while emptiness became
Anger and mistrust.

Soon she heard a beckoning
From deep inside her soul.
Hiding from her lonely heart
Began to take its toll.

Although her heart cries out to her,
She keeps it locked away.
The choice was made so long ago;
She knows no other way.

But still the heart holds onto hope
That it will be set free
When someday she finds happiness
And Love that holds the key.

ANONYMOUS

For the woman who is depressed, hopelessness, despair, and utter unworthiness can become the consuming focus of her inner life. It becomes the "truth" of her life instead of the Word of God. In the next chapter we will look more closely at how we see ourselves and treat ourselves to further expose the lies we tell ourselves and our untrue thinking patterns so that we can specifically submit them to God for healing and restoration.

The Enemy Within

Come quickly, LORD, and answer me,
for my depression deepens. Don't turn away from me,
or I will die. Let me hear of your unfailing love to me in the
morning, for I am trusting you. Show me where to walk,
for I have come to you in prayer.

PSALM 143:7-8 NLT

How precious are your thoughts about me, O God!
They are innumerable! I can't even count them;
They outnumber the grains of sand! And when I
wake up in the morning you are still with me!

PSALM 139:17-18 NLT

I, the LORD, speak the truth;
I declare what is right.

ISAIAH 45:19

For my fiftieth birthday, my friend Barb treated me to a private exercise session with her personal trainer. Prior to my individual time, the instructor invited us to participate in the class she was teaching. When I walked in, I immediately felt self-conscious. Mirrors circled an entire room filled with gorgeous young women who had toned bodies and wore the latest exercise fashions. I wore shorts and a T-shirt and felt old and frumpy. As we began to exercise, I focused on the teacher. I did not know this particular routine, and I needed to pay close attention. Whenever I glanced at the mirror and saw myself exercising, I was tempted to either laugh or cry. I looked so different than those lithe young bodies gracefully bending into the various poses. The more I kept my eyes glued on the teacher, the easier it became to focus on learning the technique. The longer I stared at myself with my imperfections, the more awful I felt.

Later on as I reflected on my morning, I realized that this was true of my inner life as well. The more I keep my eyes on Jesus, the more I will stay focused on what is true, good, and right. The more I gaze at myself in morbid introspection, the more self-conscious and depressed I will become.

Research on female mental health indicates that most women who experience depression also have poor self-esteem. Even women who don't feel particularly depressed say self-esteem and self-image problems are recurrent themes in their lives.

Why is this so? I believe one reason (of many) is that women tend to look at themselves through the mirror of their own eyes or the eyes of others, rather than through the eyes of God. When we regularly do that, we are always going to have a distorted picture of ourselves—one that will leave us feeling either vain and proud or discouraged and destroyed.

Women who are vain have inflated self-images and a great deal of self-esteem, often believing they are more important than others. On the other hand, women who see themselves negatively battle with anxiety, depressed moods, and feelings of worthlessness, inferiority, shame, and guilt. Those who think too much of themselves and those who think negatively of themselves have one thing in common: They are each centered on themselves rather than on Christ.

In order to understand how often we become our own worst enemy, let's first tackle what constitutes self-image and self-esteem, and then let's analyze what these things have to do with depression and good mental, spiritual, and relational health.

Understanding Self-Image and Self-Esteem

Our self-image is our mental picture of ourselves. Self-esteem is the way we feel about ourselves. When a woman says she has a poor self-image or low self-esteem, she usually means she doesn't like herself and doesn't see herself as a lovable, competent, or worthwhile person. Subsequently, she doesn't feel good about herself. Each of us begins to form a picture of ourselves from birth as we get a sense of how we are received and valued by those around us.

Grinning from ear to ear, Joyce recently brought me some photographs of her new granddaughter. "Isn't she beautiful?" she crooned. "Everyone is so taken with her." Baby Grace was the only girl born in several generations of children, so she became an instant celebrity.

Joyce provided the right opening to ask what her new little grandchild did to deserve such love and devotion. Puzzled, she answered, "Why would she have to do anything? She's my granddaughter. I love her just because."

Joyce gave a perfect answer to my question.

"And so," I continued, "if you, Joyce, being a mere human, can love baby Grace with such fervor, even though she cries and gets crabby and sometimes spits up all over you, why can't God love you just because?"

Joyce struggles with chronic depression and low self-esteem. Much of it has to do with the way she sees herself. Growing up, Joyce never felt loved or valued as a child. Her parents divorced when she was only five years old; her dad wasn't interested in her, and Joyce's mom was preoccupied with building a new life. Joyce's parents weren't abusive, just indifferent and busy. Joyce felt alone much of her childhood, and as a young girl she concluded she must not be worth anything and didn't deserve to be loved. She told herself that there must be something fundamentally undesirable about her that caused her parents to treat her with such neglect.

No one ever said such words directly to Joyce. Her conclusions about her value and worth came from her own perception of things as she saw herself through her parents' indifference. Joyce's picture of herself was understandable, but untrue. Her early neglect was real, but that didn't mean she was worthless or unlovable as a person, even if her parents didn't value her or love her the way she wanted them to, or even if they didn't love her at all. Rather, the situation said much more about the character of her parents and their own immaturity and sinful hearts. The consequences of her parents' sinful neglect, however, significantly impacted Joyce's life.

Looking at Joyce's early childhood, it isn't hard to see how those kinds of experiences would influence the way Joyce came to see herself (her self-image) as well as how she felt about herself (her self-esteem). Sadly, when we don't think we're worth anything to anyone and don't feel loved or important, we become a perfect candidate for depression as well as relationship problems.

Joyce's granddaughter, Grace, has the opportunity to get a different picture of herself from her first human relationships. Right from birth she is seeing herself as a much-loved and cherished child. She sees people smile at her and feels the love and warmth around her. When she cries, she is comforted and cared for. When she smiles, people who love her respond with jubilant glee. Her physical body is fed, diapered, hugged, and held. Before she can speak a word, she is forming a picture about herself that she is important and valuable to those around her and that she can trust them to care for her.

But no parents are perfect, and baby Grace is bound to experience some disappointments with the people in her world. Her parents won't always respond as quickly as she'd like when she cries. They will probably show some irritation or impatience in their voices or mannerisms when she acts crabby or whines. As Grace grows up and enters school, she won't always be treated fairly or favorably, nor will everyone always like her. What will Grace tell herself when someone doesn't think she's so cute or when she fails a test or is rejected or mocked by her friends?

Every child suffers the hard bumps that challenge a sense of worth, value, and competence. Rarely does anyone escape these years without a few deep wounds. How Grace sees herself in these experiences and then processes them in her heart will shape her mental and emotional picture of herself as well as her feelings about her abilities, value, and worth. God has charged parents with the responsibility to help their children work through these painful experiences using the wisdom he provides (see Deuteronomy 6 for an example). When that doesn't happen, or when a parent's own words or actions harm a child's spirit or body, a distorted self-image and poor self-esteem can be the result.

Consequences of a Distorted Self-Image and Poor Self-Esteem

Sometimes we mistakenly think that only those who think poorly of themselves have damaged self-images. On the contrary, many problems in life occur when we think too highly of ourselves and have an inflated self-esteem. Those who see themselves as more worthy, more special, and more deserving often treat others like second-class citizens and tend to have poor interpersonal relationships. These individuals believe that they are entitled to things that they are not entitled to and deserving of things they do not deserve. Our culture reinforces this kind of inflated thinking with the advertising slogans of "You deserve it" and "You're worth it."

When people around them don't treat them as they feel they deserve to be treated, they often become angry and depressed. A perfect example is the recent television reality program *American Idol*. Talented singers and people who want to be stars audition before three judges in hopes of becoming the next singing sensation. During the auditions, the judges shatter some of the contestants' dreams with the words, "You have the worst voice I have ever heard" or "That was terrible." Contestants who hold an inflated self-image express anger and disbelief, saying, "These judges don't know what they're talking about. Why don't they see my true worth and give me the chance that I deserve? I'm a great singer and could be the next American Idol." But everyone who heard the audition knows the real truth—although the judges could have been kinder with their words, their judgments were correct.[1]

Sadly, people with an inflated view of themselves don't always allow the harsh corrections of reality to change their thinking in order for them to develop a more truthful view of themselves—a healthier self-image. As a result, they are often prone to feeling angry, disappointed with others, and sometimes depressed because everyone doesn't see them as wonderful or as desirable or as competent as they see themselves.

Whether we see ourselves too favorably or too negatively, having a distorted self-image is not only contrary to God's best for us, but also makes many women prone to depression. Let's look at some of the long-term consequences that occur when we fail to recognize and correct this problem.

Loss of One's True Self

A woman who views herself negatively tells herself that she doesn't matter or is not worthy of love. She often denies her true feelings, even to herself. One client, Sandy, kept telling me "It doesn't matter" when I asked her how she felt when her husband, a pastor, worked long, long hours in ministry. But I knew Sandy wasn't being honest, especially with herself. It's a short walk from "it doesn't matter" to "I don't matter," and that's what Sandy was really telling herself. Sandy feared admitting her true feelings. When she was finally able to express that she felt hurt, lonely, and angry, she quickly added, "But I feel guilty for feeling that way. I'm being selfish to want his time when there are so many people who need him more. He's doing God's work. Who am I to say he should work less hours just to spend time with me?"

Sandy distanced herself from her negative feelings because they were in opposition with another internal voice that told her she was selfish and wrong to feel them in the first place. Next, guilt and shame stepped in because now that she admitted having those feelings, she saw herself as a selfish and greedy person. With all this inner turmoil going on in Sandy's heart, over time she learned it was easier to squash her honest feelings and do what she thought was expected of her.

How we deal interpersonally with such dilemmas will be covered much more extensively in chapter 9. For now, understand that Sandy's way of seeing herself contributed to how she related to her husband, as well as to others in her life. Sandy will not be able to have a constructive discussion with her husband about what bothers her until she begins to give some credibility to her real feelings and learns to fight her harsh inner critic.

Like Sandy, many women lose who they are in the context of maintaining a relationship. Fear of rejection and fear of failure keep them from being honest with themselves and others. They worry that if they are honest, it will cost them the thing they value the most—their relationships. It's easier to go along—and go along—and go along—until they are so depressed they can't go along anymore.

Like Sandy, many women remind me of a chameleon. They always change colors to match their environment, adapting and becoming what they think others want them to be in order to gain someone's attention or secure their favor. They ask themselves, *Who should I be so I can be liked; or so that I will succeed; or so that I will be perceived as a worthy, lovable, and valuable person; or a person worth listening to and spending time with?*

When a woman doesn't see herself as worth anything, this strongly influences her style of relating. She no longer knows herself or expresses what she feels or wants. She is not growing to become what God wants her to become. Rather, she becomes an expert at knowing what other people want or expect and adapts herself to meet those expectations—losing her true self in the process.

> *I tried to be everything to everybody with no thought of myself at all. I had no "self," only the self others wanted me to be. This was played out in my need to please everyone, including people at work. I had no boundaries and allowed my company and church to pile more and more on me as a manager and as a worship leader until I broke down completely.*   *~Laura*

I am a perfectionist but never good enough. I am a people pleaser, but there's always someone who's unhappy with me. I don't know how to relate with others because I always want them to like me and don't care about what I want. In general, my depression exists because I have very low self-esteem and do things in my life that guarantee that self-esteem will stay low. I have not been able to unlearn that love is conditional and that "I am not worthy."   ~ *Sarah*

Negative Self-Evaluation

Another consequence of poor self-image and negative self-esteem is that we are constantly analyzing and scrutinizing ourselves, and we're never very positive with what we see. During my exercise class, when my eyes were on the mirror instead of my instructor, I found plenty to be unhappy about. My clothes were definitely out of style, my shape was rounder than I would have liked, I was one of the oldest women in the class, and my ability to perform the exercises was minimal. If I let all of those negative thoughts and feelings have free rein, I might have left the gym before I was finished, telling myself I was stupid to go or that I looked foolish. Thankfully, in that moment, I was able to laugh at myself, accepting myself as older and rounder than the other women in the class. I put my eyes right back on my instructor so I could learn the exercises and work toward getting in better shape.

Society exerts tremendous pressure on women to be thin as well as look beautiful and youthful. Billions of dollars are spent on cosmetic surgery to achieve the "ideal" face or body. Ordinary women will never measure up to these standards. Who can afford to? But if we always tell ourselves that we should be thinner or look younger or more beautiful, or when people in our lives reinforce these lies, then we will feel constantly disappointed and insecure with ourselves because we aren't or don't, and depression may be the result.

Christian culture has some unspoken expectations for women as well; for example, we should always be nice and never hurt anyone's feelings. We should always put other people's needs and wants ahead of our own, and we must never get loud or be pushy or bossy, even if we feel angry. We should keep a beautiful and orderly home, raise successful and godly children, achieve a meaningful career or ministry, have great girlfriends, *and* make our husband really happy. Whew! I'm worn out just writing it.

Poet May Sarton, who also battled depression, said,

> I think the secret of much of the unrest and dissatisfaction with one's self and longing for a more vivid, expressive existence is the thing planted deep in everyone— turning toward the sun, the love of a virtue and splendor that must be adored. One is always trying to tune one's self to an unheard perfection. Sadly, often the perfection we're trying to tune ourselves into is a false image of the perfect self instead of God.[2]

When we measure our value and worth against our ability to maintain either our own or someone else's ideal standards, we will always fall short and suffer. No one ever stands next to "perfect" and feels good about being imperfect.

Every woman, even the one with a good self-image and positive self-esteem, battles her inner critic. Depressed women often lose this battle because the internal voice of depression is relentlessly cruel and colors her perspective on everything.

I make myself worse just by beating up on myself.
~ Pamela

I was always telling myself all the wrong things in my life were my fault.   *~ Jean*

I can't help but feel I am weak and can't cope on my own.
~ Kim

*I get negative towards myself. I let things linger and then
explode. I get very low thinking of things from my past,
what I could have done differently, or what more I could
have done and can do.*   ~ Rebekah

*My depression made me feel worse. It made me feel I am
a somewhat stupid person who has no place anywhere,
not even at church or at work. It makes me feel like a
worthless person.*   ~ Shelly

*My difficult marriage and children's problems con-
tributed to me feeling overwhelmed, although the depression and feelings of worthlessness stem from me. I still
tend to be a perfectionist and I am really hard on myself
at times. I also believe things about myself that I shouldn't
(I'm worthless, etc.) and lies from Satan, that I'm not
really saved.*   ~ Janet

The following statements are some typical things that I hear
depressed women tell themselves:

- I'm a horrible mother/wife/sister/daughter/friend/
  Christian.
- I'm fat and ugly.
- I'm a loser.
- I'm not worth anything.
- I'm stupid.
- I can't do anything right.
- I'm a failure.
- I'm a fraud.
- I'm a disappointment to everyone.
- I'm a hypocrite.

- I'm no good.
- I never measure up.
- I'm helpless.
- I'm hopeless.

When a woman who already lives with a negative self-image and poor self-esteem gets depressed, these feelings intensify and can become unbearable. The most dangerous place a woman's cruel inner critic brings her to is to believe she is helpless to change anything and it's hopeless to try. Then suicide seems like a reasonable alternative to a lifetime of pain. If you recognize that you are at this place, please call someone to help you. These feelings are too powerful for you to battle alone, and the consequences too grave if you fail. Tell your husband, pastor, best friend, a counselor, or your medical doctor, or call your local crisis hotline.

The remedy for the person with a negative self-image, as well as the person with an inflated self-image, is truth. God's Word tells us not to misjudge our value and worth, but to see ourselves truthfully— as God sees us (see Romans 12:3).

The most important question we must ask ourselves is not how I got this way, but how can I change so that I will see myself and my situations from God's perspective?

Seeing Ourselves Truthfully

We have heard this word "truth" many times thus far. That's because it is the only medicine that will heal our wounded, depressed, and sin-sick heart. Medicine is only able to do its work if we take it, and even then it usually doesn't heal us instantly. Absorbing the medicine of truth takes time. Please be patient with yourself. God knows that pure truth is often too potent to be administered alone. Truth must always be mixed with grace and love, and the Lord usually gives us small amounts of truthful medicine to start. Just as we need to take certain medicines for the rest of our lives, the healing elixir of truth isn't only taken when we're sick. We need daily doses of it to help us stay healthy and grow.

The Bible says that our heart automatically leans toward believing lies over truth (Jeremiah 8:5; 17:9; Romans 1:25). We don't intentionally plant lies in our heart, but like weeds in our flower garden, they are there. And just as weeds mar the beauty of a garden, lies and deception (whether it be self-deception or lies told to us) ruin a soul. In his bestselling book *The Road Less Traveled,* psychiatrist Scott Peck said, "One of the roots of mental illness is invariably an interlocking system of lies that we have been told and lies we tell ourselves."[3]

When we believe lies about ourselves, lies about God, lies about life, lies about how to handle problems, and lies about others, we become mentally, emotionally, and spiritually ill. To become healthy, we must first identify these lies and then renounce them for what they are. This process needs to be done regularly because, like weeds, many lies we have believed have deep roots that are not easily killed.

As we grow to see things more truthfully about ourselves, God, others, and life, the next step is figuring out how to live in that different reality. For example, how do I live as a woman of dignity and value? How should I handle myself when I fail or disappoint myself? How do I speak the truth in love to others when they hurt me? How do I draw close to God when I no longer see him as a harsh judge or as a disinterested Deity, but rather as a loving Father who enjoys me? Learning to believe these truths is the first step; living from them takes time and practice. As in most other things, the more consistently we apply what we are learning to real-life situations, the more we will gain confidence and become better with those situations.

God's Word is the only true mirror that accurately reflects who we are and how we are to see ourselves. Just as I needed to stop staring at myself in the mirror and keep my eyes on my exercise instructor in order to stay focused and make progress, we need to keep our eyes on God and his Word as our means of seeing ourselves and our situation truthfully. The battle you face right now is which voice you will listen to and trust to be your truest truth. Will it be God's Word or the negative voices in your own head and heart? The following truth is foundational in starting to correct your self-image:

> **God loves you because he chooses to,
> not because you are worthy of his love or deserve it.**

At first glance, this may sound shocking to those of us who have been fed a steady diet of psychobabble, but in reality, once you grasp this truth, it is quite freeing. Authentic love is always a gift, not a reward for good behavior or something we can earn.

Many depressed women say, "I wish I could believe God loves me, but I can't because I don't feel worthy. Help me feel worthy." The internal lie is *I must be or feel worthy in order to receive love*. This is a common deception in depression as well as in women with low self-esteem. We all want to feel worthy and deserving. That would make us feel good about ourselves and boost our sagging self-images. Here's one woman's struggle to get free from this lie:

> *I believe that God is loving and forgiving and that nothing I have done or will do can change that. I believe that my name is in the "Book of Life," but I'd rather keep proving that I am worthy enough to be there for some reason. Old habits!*   ~ Sarah

Let's first take a look at this lie on the human level. Do we love our children because they deserve to be loved or are worthy of it? If the answer is yes, we love them *because* they are worthy and deserving, then what about those children who aren't loved? The day after Joyce shared with me the good news about her granddaughter, another baby girl washed up dead on the New Jersey shore. Was Grace *more* worthy to be loved than that abandoned infant? Absolutely not! Every child is a gift from God and should be received and valued as such. If someone gives me a diamond bracelet and I throw it in the trash, does that act make the bracelet less valuable? No, it makes me a fool.

Along the same line, my husband, Howard, does not love me because I deserve it. In fact, many times I don't deserve his love. He loves me because he wants to, not because I'm worthy. And if he didn't want to love me someday, it would not be because I was no longer worthy. My worth has nothing to do with it. Love is a choice. It cannot be coerced or forced, bought or earned. It is a gift from the one who loves to the beloved. In the Bible the stories of Hosea and Gomer (see the Old Testament book of Hosea) and the prodigal son (Luke 15:11-32) richly demonstrate how *undeserving* the one who is loved can be. Love cannot be something that is deserved, otherwise it isn't genuine love.

It's true that people don't always love us the way we'd like them to or as much as we want them to. Rejection hurts, but rejection is not a statement about our true worth or value. Let's look at this from a slightly different angle. Suppose I went around telling everyone who didn't love me the way I'd like them to that I deserved to be loved and valued by them because I was worthy and deserving of it. Love never works that way. I think if I acted like that, everyone would rightly think I was quite full of myself and be turned off.

Perhaps someone you loved told you that you were a burden or a mistake. Careless words wound a person's spirit and can be extremely painful. But please hear me. *Even if your parents or your husband or everyone you know treated you horribly, you are still a person of value. You have eternal significance.* How do I know this? Because your heavenly Father, your Creator, God Almighty, declares this to be so (Matthew 10:31; 12:12; Ephesians 2:10). He loves you fully and completely—not because you are cute or talented or perfect or worthy. He loves you because he chooses to love you.

C.S. Lewis says, "The value of the individual does not lie in him. He is capable of receiving value. He receives it by union with Christ."[4] We do not affirm ourselves by believing we deserve God's love (or anyone else's love), or telling ourselves over and over again that we are worthy of love. Almighty God affirms us (read Psalm 139 for the psalmist's experience of this affirmation).

There is great comfort in knowing that God loves us because he is God and not because we're worthy of it or deserve it. We're as helpless to earn God's love as Joyce's grandbaby was to earn her family's love. They loved her because they wanted to. In the same way, but even more so, God loves us just because—because he is God. God's nature is love; therefore, he cannot *not* love us. There is nothing you can ever do to earn or deserve God's love, and there is nothing you can ever do to lose or lessen it.[5] The love of God is active, relentlessly pursuing you, seeking your good, fighting for your eternal well-being. His love is perfect and sufficient, never more and never less than it always is (Romans 8:31-39).

The Bible tells us that God loved us when we were at our absolute worst (Romans 5:8), and Jesus tells us that the Father loves us as much as the Father loved him (John 17:23). The reality and security of God's love does not depend upon us at all. David Powlison wisely writes, "God does not accept me just as I am; he loves me *despite* how I am."[6] What a relief! The apostle John encourages us with these words: "We know and *rely* on the love God has for us. God is love. Whoever lives in love lives in God, and God in him" (1 John 4:16, emphasis added).

Listen to the words of other women who learned to rest on this truth for themselves:

> *I've tried to focus on the fact that God made me and that he loves me just as I am. The more in tune I am to God making me special, the more I can accept myself.*
> ~ *Pamela*

> *Throughout my life I had always felt God's presence with me, but I felt so unworthy that the God of the universe could love me. Now I accept myself as his precious child, not a throwaway or reject.*   ~ *Laura*

I have learned that I am very hard on myself. I also let others take advantage of me. Sometimes I don't take very good care of myself. I almost expect others to mistreat me, and I've actually been allowing it. I've also learned that God understands all these things and still loves me more than I realized.   ~Cindy

I am grateful for God's mercy in my life. Without the knowledge of the unconditional love of God, I would likely be a drunk prostitute right now.   ~Audrey

We always see ourselves in the light of another, but it is not our own light or the light of another person by which we right ourselves. To correct our damaged self-image and low self-esteem, we must take our eyes off ourselves and put them on the one and only true light, God. He shows us how to rightly view ourselves. Listen to Wendy and Rebecca share how believing God has begun to make a difference in their lives:

I'm learning that God loves me and wants the best for me, that I can seek the best for myself, and that it is okay to feel good about myself.   ~Wendy

If it were not for the work of the Holy Spirit and God's Word, I would not make it. When I am ugly (impatient and harsh and self-centered), my pride wants to help me weasel out of true repentance, and my sorrow and feelings of failure make me want to sink into self-pity or bang my head against the wall and hurt myself. The Holy Spirit keeps me honest (no excuses), while at the same time God's Word promises me hope—"There is therefore now no condemnation to those who are in Christ Jesus" (Romans 8:1 NKJV). The Bible has many more promises and teachings to help me keep going.
                                                    ~Rebecca

The Power of Words

Something to Think About

The minute Maggie walked into the office, I saw the pain in her eyes. Earlier in the week her mother said some cruel words to her and now she couldn't get them out of her mind. I wasn't surprised at how quickly her mother's harsh words undid her. Maggie slipped into familiar habits, became depressed, and told herself she was a failure as a daughter, a sister, a mother, and a wife.

As young girls we grew up chanting the old nursery rhyme. *Sticks and stones will break our bones, but words will never hurt us.* That is a lie. Words are powerful, even words that aren't true. The Bible tells us that words can wound us (Proverbs 12:18) and words can heal us (Psalm 107:20; Proverbs 16:24). Words affect our emotions (Proverbs 12:25; 15:1) and our body (Psalm 119:25). What words do you most regularly say to yourself? Encouraging words? Healing words? True words? God's words? Whatever words you feed on will be the ones that nourish your heart. The psalmist cries out in his anguish, "My soul is weary with sorrow; strengthen me according to your word" (Psalm 119:28).

Jesus wants us to realize that "it takes more than bread to stay alive. It takes a steady stream of words from God's mouth" (Matthew 4:4 MSG). Begin to feed yourself true words, the words of God. He is the only one who *always* tells us the truth and *always* loves us.

Something to Do

How did you feel when you read that God loves you because he chooses to? Were you uncomfortable? Did you feel relieved? Sad?

Hopeful? Angry? Happy? Write down any negative thoughts that came to your mind.

For example, one of my clients wrote, "Yeah, right. If God loves me, he's sure got a great way of showing me." Another wrote, "I wish I could believe that, but I can't." Keep writing down all your negative thoughts and feelings until you don't have any more. Looking at your negative thoughts and feelings will help you find the lies that keep you from believing what God tells you.

Each time you identify a lie, you must renounce it. Call it a lie and tell yourself what the truth is. For example, if the lie is "I need to be worthy to receive God's love," tell yourself the truth: "I'm not worthy of his love, but he gives it to me anyway. Though I am not deserving of his love, I am not worthless. I am a person of value and worth because he declares me to be so as his creation and as his child."

Next pray the verses that support these truths out loud. You will find a treasury of helpful Scripture verses starting on page 235. Another wonderful resource that will help you pray through all kinds of problems using Scripture is *Praying God's Word* by Beth Moore. This begins the process of uniting God's truth with a heart willing to receive it. You may not yet be totally convinced of the trustworthiness of God's character, but you can, by faith, choose to trust it anyway. We do this every day when we choose to put our trust in a cab driver we don't know to safely take us somewhere or a doctor to give us the right medicine when we're sick. In many ways we choose to take a step of faith and trust, even when we're not sure. Faith is a decision our will makes—even when our feelings are reluctant or negative.

Take that leap of faith and tell God you are willing to believe his words over your own internal words. Start to internalize his Word every day into your heart. Begin by saying the following truth out loud and write it at the beginning of your journal entries for a week. Ask God to help you believe it with your whole heart.

> Long ago, even before he made the world, God loved [me] and chose [me] in Christ to be holy and without fault in his eyes. His unchanging plan has always been to adopt [me] into his family by bringing [me] to himself through Jesus Christ. And this gave him great pleasure (Ephesians 1:4-5 NLT).

This is good news for you! God finds pleasure in you. He chose you and adopted you into his family. Can you imagine how wonderful it would feel if you could simply rest in the truth of his Word? The psalmist said, "In his word I put my hope" (Psalm 130:5). Will you?

Hope for When Life Becomes Too Hard

And now my life ebbs away; Days of suffering grip me.
Night pierces my bones; My gnawing pains never rest.
In his great power, God becomes like clothing to me;
he binds me like the neck of my garment. He throws me
into the mud, and I am reduced to dust and ashes.
I cry out to you, O God, but you do not answer;
I stand up, but you merely look at me.
JOB 30:16-20

The LORD helps the fallen
and lifts up those bent beneath their loads.
PSALM 145:14 NLT

I live in a rural area surrounded by rolling hills. I have a spectacular view and a great walking workout route. On most warm days I trek to the main road and back, a total of about four miles. It's a strenuous walk up and down hilly terrain, but that's a good way to guarantee an aerobic challenge and an excellent leg workout.

My road is not only hilly, it is also very windy. With the wind at my back, I feel an invisible force pushing me along. Exercising feels effortless; at those times I even start jogging. Other times it's not so easy. When the wind faces me, it whips my body and opposes my every step. Climbing up those hills hurts, and occasionally I give up and don't finish the entire loop.

Some days the wind roars into a furious storm. The temperature drops and rain starts to pound. When that happens, my walk feels unbearable. Four miles seems like ten and the 60 minutes it normally takes feels like hours. When I finally reach home, my muscles ache, my head hurts, and all I want to do is crawl into bed.

Life is a lot like that. A little hardship gives us challenges to overcome and builds good emotional and relational resilience. But when extra difficulty is added, it often depletes our energy and drains our resources. Overwhelming and chronic stress pushes us over the edge, breaks us down, and makes us sick.

> *When I was depressed, I didn't know how to handle stress; it handled me and drove me further into depression. Today, I try to determine if stress is good or bad. Good stress is constructive, keeping me focused and helping me get things done. Bad stress, like bad guilt, only adds to destructive thinking, which leads to destructive behavior.*
>
> *~Laura*

> *Stress made me depressed. Over the past two or three years, my natural father died after a battle with cancer. He lived far away, and even though we said our good-byes, I wasn't able to help like I thought I should. In fact, the depression kicked in after a visit with my stepmother to check on her. In addition, my maternal grandfather died, and my grandmother's health steadily deteriorated so that my mom had to take care of her in her home. All those things, in addition to being the wife of a pastor, working full-time in ministry, and having two children in college, were too much.*   *~Veda*

Causes of Stress

It's important that a woman recognize the causes of her stress and how to implement preventive or corrective measures so that she will take good care of herself and, if possible, not allow herself to become totally depleted. There are two main causes of stress: those that come from external sources and those that come from within. When we feel stressed-out or overwhelmed, it is often a combination of both causes at work.

Life's Difficulties

This summer I taught counseling classes at a Bible institute in Siberia, Russia. One of my students approached me about her friend Rhonda, who appeared depressed. She asked if I would be willing to speak with her.

Rhonda was a teacher, but recent health difficulties had made it impossible for her to work. Her husband was a cruel man who drank too much. He spent much of the family's income on alcohol, leaving Rhonda scrambling to find money to buy food and to pay bills. Russia does not have social programs in place that might help women like Rhonda. She also had no extended family nearby. Rhonda felt desperate, and she was in despair. From her perspective, God had failed her. Her husband didn't love her. Her family couldn't help her. Her children needed her, but she couldn't help them—she was too overwhelmed.

In these kinds of situations, where there is an avalanche of difficulties, I'm always puzzled when people say, "God never gives us more than we can handle." Oh no? Try telling that to Rhonda or to Job or to the apostle Paul. It is often during these times that a woman who normally has very good coping abilities and relational strengths is most vulnerable to depression. One author puts it this way, "Many, not naturally inclined to melancholy, have, by overwhelming and repeated calamities, been sunk into this dark gulf."[1]

The Bible assures us of many things, but it never promises that we won't be slammed with overwhelming hardship. In fact, Jesus says just the opposite (John 16:33). Job's ten children were killed in an accident, his financial resources were wiped out, and his health failed, all within a span of a few weeks. In addition to physical and emotional pain, the endless negativity and criticism from Job's wife and friends added more stress to his broken heart and weakened body.

It's no wonder that he said he'd rather die than continue to live that way (Job 7:15).

The apostle Paul said he suffered hardships "beyond our ability to endure." It was so much that he too "despaired even of life" (2 Corinthians 1:8). One of the highest risk factors for depression is recent stressful events and life's difficulties.[2] When things that are beyond our control start careening out of control, what can we do so that we aren't swallowed up in a black hole of despair?

Like Rhonda or Job, we may not be able to change what's going on in our life. We feel stressed-out, anxious, and even desperate. Yet we do have a choice to make. In the midst of these difficulties and in spite of our emotions, we can choose to put our hope in God.

I find most people who put their hope in God hope he will do something to make their situation better. When that doesn't happen (and sometimes it doesn't), they lose hope and become angry with him. That happened to Jeremiah. While mourning over the devastation of Israel, Jeremiah became angry with God and lost hope (Lamentations 3:18). Later his hope rekindled, but it wasn't hope that God was going to do something. Instead, it was hope in who God was, hope in his character (Lamentations 3:21-25). The psalmist also reminded himself to put his hope in God's character in the midst of his despair (Psalm 42:5).

Melissa knew firsthand how this hope works. Life had been particularly difficult that week. Already depressed, her heart began filling with anxiety and dread. She tried calling me for some extra reassurance, but I wasn't in the office, nor did I return her phone call. In addition to being highly stressed, Melissa began to feel hurt and abandoned by me. She told herself that I didn't really care about her, she was a bother to me, and I didn't want to help her. The more she told herself these negative thoughts, the worse she felt. Then she caught herself and chose (her will) to practice some of the things we had been talking about in our counseling. She talked to herself, asking herself what evidence she had to indicate that I was uncaring and unresponsive. She told herself that I always returned previous phone calls and showed care for her in many ways in the past. She knew me as a kind, honest, and caring person. She stopped her negative thinking and started talking differently to herself. She said, "I don't know why Leslie is not returning my phone call. But I know it's not because she doesn't care or that she doesn't want to help me. She's not like that. That's not who she is." She was able to experience some reassurance in the midst of her stressful week and hurt emotions by remembering my character, even though my unresponsiveness at the moment confused her.

When life is hard and everything looks bleak, the Bible encourages us to put our hope in God's character (Psalm 119:68). We hope in his loving-kindness, his grace, his sovereignty, and his wisdom, even when we don't understand his ways. What other hope do we have? Hope in God is the only hope that is strong enough to create an eye to sustain us in life's hurricane. Without the hope that God is good and he is who he says he is, the pain of life can become overwhelming. (And one of Satan's strongest ploys is to get us to doubt God's goodness and his love.) One of my favorite Scripture passages was penned by a man who hoped in God while the hardships of life crashed upon him. He wrote:

> Though the fig tree does not bud and there are no grapes on the vines, though the olive crop fails and the fields produce no food, though there are no sheep in the pen and no cattle in the stalls, yet I will rejoice in the LORD, I will be joyful in God my Savior. The Sovereign LORD is my strength; he makes my feet like the feet of a deer, he enables me to go on the heights (Habakkuk 3:17-19).

Because God loves us, he often sends us comforters, friends, and compassionate people to help carry us when life becomes too much. He may not change situations the way we'd like him to, but often his comforting arms and resources of help are sent through others who reach out to you. Rhonda needed her friend to give her perspective, comfort her in her despair, and remind her that God still loved her.

God also used her friend to bring groceries, help pay some bills, and take her to the doctor. Job said, "A despairing man should have the devotion of his friends" (Job 6:14), and the apostle Paul said that God comforted him in his depression by sending Titus (2 Corinthians 7:5-7). The book of Ecclesiastes reminds us of the importance of our relationships with others when it says, "Two are better than one, because they have a good return for their work: If one falls down, his friend can help him up. But pity the man who falls and has no one to help him up!" (Ecclesiastes 4:9-10).

When someone loves you, they want to help you carry burdens that are too big for you to carry alone (Galatians 6:2). I have seen the worst of times transformed into some of the best of times because of the close, caring comfort of loving friends. Don't tell yourself that you have to be in this situation all alone. When life becomes overwhelming, don't isolate yourself. Tell a friend you trust. Allow others to help and be there for you. Take a moment right now and think of three people who care about you. Allow yourself to feel the warmth that comes from knowing you are loved.

Life is not only difficult because of things that happen to us. Life often feels stressful because of the pressure we put on ourselves. This stress is caused by internal problems such as worry, wrong thinking, unexpressed feelings, and irrational and unrealistic expectations of ourselves. We've already talked about how negative and wrong thinking, as well as not listening to our true feelings, can lead to depression. When we fail to live up to our own idealized version of ourselves, we not only feel disappointed in ourselves, but we often also hate ourselves and become depressed.

Unrealistic Expectations of Yourself

In chapter 5 we learned how our picture of ourselves (self-image) shapes our feelings about ourselves (self-esteem). During childhood we may attempt to boost our low self-esteem by putting certain expectations or standards on ourselves that we try to live up to. Sometimes we sense that significant others in our lives are more pleased with us or seem to love us more when we achieve certain things (like good grades) or make them happy. When we succeed, we feel good about ourselves; when we fail, we don't.

For many of us, the standards we try to maintain are impossible, causing internal pressure and stress in two ways. First, we knock ourselves out trying to live up to some impossible ideal image we've constructed just to feel normal. Second, we become disappointed and beat ourselves up when we fail to measure up to this ideal image.

Most depressed women I've worked with believe any number of the following lies. They include these:

1. I have to be perfect or make everything perfect for everyone else to feel happy and/or to be accepted and loved.

2. I have to do it all because the harder I work and the more I do, the better I feel about myself and the more I will be valued, loved, and accepted.

3. I have to make other people happy and please them because then they will need me, like me more, and want me around.

Let's look at how these lies lay the foundation for depression to take root.

Shortly after Sandy's birth, her mom was hospitalized for postpartum depression. Sandy's father, overwhelmed by the responsibilities of providing for six children, rarely came home from work. Baby Sandy's care fell on her oldest sister, who was 16 years old and not exactly thrilled about this new responsibility. She tried to care for the baby the best she could, but deep down she resented Sandy for her mom's illness and for wrecking her social life. When Sandy cried, she often was yelled at, and she spent a lot of time left alone in her crib. Sandy was fed regularly, but usually with a bottle propped up against a pillow instead of being nestled in a loving arm. Rarely did anyone play or smile at Sandy. No one took her picture as a baby. Although no one said it directly, Sandy grew up seeing herself as the cause of her mother's illness and the family's distress. She told herself she had ruined everyone's life, and she felt guilty she was even born. Sandy tried hard to be a good girl. She told herself that if she were perfect, maybe her father and her siblings would love her and pay attention to her. Sandy's mental picture of herself and her feelings about herself were deeply influenced by these early experiences.

When Sandy entered school, she continued to work hard at being perfect and began to receive attention and admiration from her peers and teachers for her academic achievement. She was also pretty and boys began to notice her. As her natural abilities and physical attractiveness were affirmed, Sandy began to feel more worthwhile and competent. This isn't necessarily a bad thing, but no one is successful and desirable to everyone all of the time. When Sandy's physical attractiveness didn't measure up to her standards for herself or her achievements or personality didn't win the attention or affirmation she craved, she fell apart. Her self-esteem (sense of well-being) depended upon maintaining her image of herself as a beautiful woman who did everything well and made everyone happy (all of the time).

Like Sandy, many of us have developed a false self, one that tries to earn the love and approval of others by being good enough, pretty enough, productive enough, or perfect enough. Women who live this way are self-conscious and anxious about the imagined disapproval of others. They frequently berate themselves (their internal critic) for falling short of what they thought they or others thought they should be. Striving to meet these unrealistic expectations and pressures takes its toll on our bodies and our emotions, and provides additional ammunition to the negative and untrue thoughts we may believe about ourselves. These negative patterns create a perfect environment for chronic stress and episodes of depression to flourish.

When we live this way, we are not able to become the person God created us to be. We won't grow because we're afraid to fail and don't try something new because we feel stupid if we're not sure we can do it perfectly—the first time. When we define our worth and value through the approval and acceptance of others, what happens to us when people don't think we're important enough to spend time with or valuable enough to give their love? When we are always measuring ourselves against some perfect ideal of ourselves, or what we think others want or expect us to be, we stunt our own growth as a person.

Many women put unrealistic expectations on themselves to do it all, be it all, and have it all. We live in a frenzied world where our body is constantly pumping adrenaline just to keep up. It's little wonder why we feel irritable, intolerant, and moody. The external stress of life's hardships isn't the only thing that flattens our spirits. The internal stress, the things we put on ourselves, can push us over the brink as well. We tell ourselves we should be a Betty Crocker mom, a Victoria's Secret wife, and a Martha Stewart housekeeper, all while working to help provide some family income. We ought to home-school our kids and feel guilty if we don't want to or can't. We should pray and study our Bible every day, take care of our aging parents, get more involved in church, work out at the gym…the list goes on and on. Something has to give. Before we realize it, we are feeling as though life is one gigantic hamster wheel. We're not sure how we got on or how to get off without causing the entire empire we've created to collapse.

> *I've always lived as if I could do it all—or should. I knew I wasn't superwoman but thought I was supposed to be. I guess I've been depressed for years—I just didn't know it because I was still functioning. It was only when I couldn't get out of bed, and didn't even care if I did, that I got scared.* ~Karen

The truth is you are not perfect. You can't do it all or please everyone all of the time. We will look at this issue more fully as it relates to our relationships with others in chapters 8 and 9. For now, let's take some first steps on ways to decrease our stress.

How to Manage and Reduce Stress

Something to Think About

Stress overload is a contributing factor in most cases of depression. In our hectic, fast-paced lives, we are faced with hundreds of choices a day from simple to complex. The demands of deciphering all of one's choices can become overwhelming, especially if we tell ourselves we can never make a mistake because we must be perfect. How we manage our stress and teach ourselves to de-stress can make the difference.

I don't think I ever really pondered what it means to "handle stress." I think I equate handling stress with surviving it. I don't think I've ever consciously considered a game plan for dealing with stress, as in alleviating it. Although, "escaping" when I'm feeling extremely overwhelmed would probably fit into that category. I would escape when I was younger by hopping on my bicycle and riding to a quiet place, just riding or getting lost in music. Alcohol has also been a form of trying to escape, but it doesn't really work. Now I go for a ride in my van to a favorite quiet place, getting lost in music or prayer, or I go for a walk. The newest addition to "stress busting" would be my 75-pound heavy bag I can "beat the tar out of" if I feel like exploding. ~Diane

Something to Do

Here are four things you can learn to do in order to prevent life from getting the best of you. As you learn to do these things and practice them, you will find you are better able to handle stress instead of feeling overwhelmed by it. Read through each item, but pick only one of them to practice for now. After you've implemented one of these new habits consistently, come back and pick another. Over time you will build good coping skills so that you can manage stress in a healthier way.

1. TAKE BETTER CARE OF YOUR BODY

One of the best ways to help your body de-stress is to teach it how to relax. When you are anxious or in pain, your muscles tighten, your body feels tense, and your emotions are agitated. Medication may help as a temporary measure, but there are no good long-term medications for anxiety.

There are relaxation techniques that can help you lower your physical tension as well as emotional stress. But you must learn how to use them—and that is not as easy as it seems. When I was pregnant, my husband and I signed up for Lamaze class to prepare for natural childbirth. I attended the class and learned everything I could, but I didn't practice. I told myself it was so easy I didn't need to. I was wrong. As childbirth progressed, I could not concentrate or focus on relaxing my body. I hadn't trained my muscles to respond to my mental commands or imagery, so when the pain of labor was upon me, all my head knowledge was useless to me. As with any other skill you are learning, repeated and regular practice is required for you to learn how to relax your body.

There are many good books and tapes that will teach you how to do progressive relaxation. You can find them online or at a bookstore. If you are very depressed, relaxation exercises may make your body feel more lethargic. Moderate walking may be more helpful to you.

Something simple that everyone does unconsciously is breathe. When we're stressed-out and anxious, our breathing is often shallow and rapid. Learning how to breathe deeply can help you relax your body and mind and bring a heightened sense of well-being. The physiological changes that deep breathing produces can counter some of the negative effects of stress on your body. Once you get the hang of it, you can do it anywhere, and no one will notice that you are doing it.

At first, lie down with your knees bent and your back pressed into the floor. Place one hand on your abdomen, the other on your chest. Breathe in slowly through your nose and feel your belly fill with air. Your chest should only move a little bit. Exhale through your mouth, gently blowing out. Purposefully relax your mouth, jaw, and tongue as you exhale. Continue this gentle, rhythmic breathing in through your nose, out through your mouth, for about five to ten minutes at a time. Try to focus only on your breathing. Listen to how it sounds and pay attention to your body as you deeply breathe in and breathe out. Practice this exercise once or twice daily for four to six weeks until it is engrained into your body memory.

Once you've learned how deep breathing feels, you can do it inconspicuously while waiting in a long line, driving in a snarled traffic jam, or anytime you feel tense or stressed in order to relax your body and your mind.

Acute stress triggers our adrenal system to release powerful hormones into our body to prepare us for fight or flight. When prolonged, these hormones can damage our cardiovascular system as well as cause other health problems. Chronic stress has been linked to immune problems, impaired memory, and weakened bones. When under stress, the body releases cortisol, a stress hormone, which causes carbohydrate cravings, leading to weight gain. Cortisol is relatively harmless in small doses but does serious harm to our bodies when pumped continuously into our system. Therefore it is critical that we learn ways to de-stress.

Some women find it difficult to carve out time alone to refresh themselves, whether it be physically, emotionally, or spiritually. We tend to be givers and tell ourselves we're selfish if we make time for ourselves, yet appropriate self-love and godly self-care is not selfish, but essential. Jesus told his disciples after a particularly hectic day of ministry, "Come with me by yourselves to a quiet place and get some rest" (Mark 6:31). It is only when we are healthy physically, mentally, emotionally, and spiritually that we are best able to give of ourselves to care for and encourage others. When we are depleted ourselves, we don't have much to offer anyone else.

> *I learned that our body really is a temple...and if we exercise, eat right, and drink enough water, it really helps.*   *~Joy*

> *I try to relax, exercise, and talk it out sometimes.*
> *~Connie*

> *Before I got depressed, I got enough sleep, took vitamins, and went to the doctor regularly for checkups, but my eating habits were borderline and I did not enjoy exercising. Now I am making myself a priority. I am eating better, and I have started to exercise regularly, do cardio work, and do strength training. I have found out that I enjoy my workouts and look forward to them. ~Karen*

2. ACCEPT YOUR LIMITATIONS

We must emotionally accept the fact that we are human beings. That may sound odd, but many of us try to ignore that reality. We refuse to accept that we are finite, limited people who don't know everything, can't do everything, aren't perfect, need sleep, get sick, and sometimes do wrong.

I'm not saying anything you don't already know, but knowing it and accepting it are two different things. Listen to your self-talk when you are faced with the reality of your limitations. Do you say, "I should have known better" or "I should have been able to stop that from happening"? If so, you believe the lie that you should be all-knowing and all-powerful.

Do you berate yourself for your sins and mistakes? Then perhaps, on one hand, you acknowledge that you're not perfect but emotionally won't accept it. Debbie came to counseling, extremely depressed. Her husband had left her because of her affair. "How could I have done such an awful thing?" she lamented. It wasn't only her failed marriage she grieved; Debbie felt devastated and ashamed that she did not live up to her own ideal image of herself as a good Christian wife. Her wounded pride was depressing her more than the loss of her marriage.

When you can't emotionally accept that you're a sinner, you can't emotionally accept God's forgiveness or his help. Instead, you tell yourself that you shouldn't need it because you should be better than that. Accepting our humanity means we know, accept, and live within our limits. We don't try to play God or be God. We recognize that we need more than ourselves to manage our life successfully. We need God. That awareness is good because then we can run to the God who loves us and wants us even when we mess up. He doesn't condemn us the way we are prone to condemn ourselves (Romans 8:1). Rather, he forgives us and helps us to change so that we grow to become a holy (whole) person.

In addition to accepting our limitations, we must also learn to accept that we are not all the same. We have different gifts, temperaments, and preferences. One of my girlfriends ran a day care in her home. For her, a roomful of loud, playful children was energizing and fun; I ended up with a pounding headache. I didn't feel guilty that I wasn't as thrilled with taking care of kids as she was. I recognized those were not my gifts or interests and went home. Too many women don't accept who they are. Instead, they continuously compare themselves with others, always coming up short. They think they should like what other women like, do what other women do, and feel what other women feel. When you are always trying to be like someone else or what you think other people want you to be instead of being who God made you to be, you will feel drained and stressed-out, perhaps taking on things that God did not intend for you to do.

Here again are the words of real women who battled accepting their own limitations:

I hate stress. Lately, I have been turning off the faucets that cause me stress. I upset people by letting them know I'm unable to help them, and I disappoint even myself sometimes because I can't do all the wonderful things I want to do. But before I used to take on everything until my hair stood up straight. Now, I still take on too much, but when I feel myself going overboard, I withdraw from my least favorite activities, no matter who gets mad.

~*Audrey*

The gift in carrying depression around is in getting to know your limits. I can only make my own choices (on a good day). I can't control others. I can learn to put up good boundaries, and go through the grief of letting people go who are not choosing to be a part of my life.

~*Vickki*

I realized I didn't have to do it all myself...I hired a cleaning lady, who really frees up my time, letting me relax and read magazines in my spare time.   ~*Joy*

I am learning to let go of the little things that stress me out. Life is not as difficult as I make it sometimes, and my need to "control" people, places, and things is slowly dissipating. I have a very long way to go with this one.

~*Sarah*

I take much more time out to take care of me. I try not
to push myself so hard and to accept myself. To focus on
God being in control.   *~Pam*

3. PRIORITIZE YOUR RESOURCES

We only have four resources at our disposal. They are our time, talents, energy, and money. We often overspend these finite resources on things that aren't really important, leaving us with no margin for emergencies or fun. How we choose to allocate our resources of time, talents, energy, and money not only impacts us, but also those we love. It is essential that we give some thought to our deepest values and priorities.

Feeling stressed-out often exposes how we have been misspending our resources. For example, many people are overwhelmed these days because of high credit card debt and financial difficulties. Their resource of money has been overspent, and the consequences are now draining them emotionally and financially.

We can do the same thing with our other resources. We go into debt with our energy and talent resources by extending ourselves over and over again beyond our limits, leaving ourselves physically drained and emotionally exhausted. Always hurrying is a refusal to accept the reality of time. We leave no margins for interruptions or delays and try to squeeze every moment out of our day. It's not surprising that we feel like a taut rubber band ready to snap.

Sometimes life becomes too hard because we have not been good stewards of our resources. We collapse under the stress of trying to do more than we have the resources to handle. Take some time to evaluate how you allocate your resources of time, talents, energy, and money. Ask yourself these questions:

- Are you living within your limits, or are you always over-drawn?

- Do you budget your resources according to your values and priorities and your family's needs, or do you use up your resources in order to live up to others' expectations or gain their approval?

I'm more careful about not overloading my schedule with lots of busyness. This gives me much needed quiet time at home.   ~ Gina

I am much more proactive. When stress hits, I see it as an enemy to be subdued so it won't turn into depression.
                                                  ~ Trish

I have to watch for signs of trouble and instability, like overextending myself. I have learned to say no and not allow persons, places, or things to break my step, speed, or relationship with the Father.   ~ Ellen

1. LEARN TO GET QUIET WITH GOD

In our time-starved, get-more-done world, many of us never take a moment to be quiet and still in God's presence. When we're feeling good, it may seem like a waste of time. When we're not feeling good, our anxious thoughts and emotional turmoil make it hard to get quiet.

The psalmist tells us to "be still in the presence of the LORD, and wait patiently for him to act" (Psalm 37:7 NLT). Christian meditation and prayer can help us remember what is true and restore a sense of peace when our negative thoughts threaten to overwhelm us. When I'm stressed-out, I love meditating on the first few verses of Psalm 23. Listen to the words and picture yourself in the moment the psalmist describes:

> The LORD is my shepherd; I have everything I need. He lets me rest in green meadows; He leads me beside peaceful streams. He renews my strength (verses 1-3 NLT).

Close your eyes and imagine yourself lying in a grassy field right near a gentle bubbling brook. Feel the sun warm your skin. Take a deep breath and smell the clean air and wild meadow grass. Listen as the birds chirp their hymns. As you quietly lie there, do nothing but rest and breathe deeply, reminding yourself that God is your Shepherd. He provides everything you need. In this moment, he renews your strength. He replenishes your resources. The New International Version says, "He restores my soul" (verse 3).

Stay quiet and let the Lord's strength flow into your body, spirit, heart, and mind. Often it is during these quiet times of being still that the Holy Spirit has a chance to change the way I see my difficulties and remind me of God's faithfulness. That may be exactly what I need in order to cope more effectively with my situation.

I spend time in God's presence. I exercise. I try to adapt my lifestyle so that I do not have a lot of stress.   ~Stacy

I try to spend time with the Lord rather than requiring myself to keep up with my normal pace of activities— I give myself some grace and actively pursue what the Lord is trying to show me in this situation.   ~Anna

Here is a short prayer you might say when you are feeling stressed or beaten up by life. Sit very still and get quiet, breathing in and out. Depression often robs us of our ability to think or remember, so write this prayer out on a small index card and tuck it into your pocket or purse. Then it will be handy when you need it.

A Prayer from My Heart

Lord, grant me faith, dispel doubt
Give me hope, take away despair
Fill me with love, remove fear.

During these quiet, still times, God works to change the stress that is crippling us into something that can actually strengthen us.

Remember these stress-busters:

- Learn to prioritize and say no when you need to.
- Slow down and stop living your life in a hurry.
- Stop procrastinating. It causes stress because things get backed up.
- Remember that you're not God and are not omnipotent.
- Meditate on God's perspective and his character.
- Let go of what you cannot control and change.
- Practice deep breathing and learn relaxation.
- Have fun and enjoy the little things of life—beauty, nature, music.
- Exercise—burn off that extra adrenaline.

Part Two

A Woman's Relationship with Others

Redeeming
the Past

I will save you from the hands of the wicked
And redeem you from the grasp of the cruel.
JEREMIAH 15:21

He has sent me to bind up the
brokenhearted, to proclaim freedom
for the captives and release from
darkness for the prisoners.
ISAIAH 61:1

Tamar's life as a child seemed idyllic. She lived in extravagance with servants at her beck and call, the daughter of a wealthy and influential father. Although Tamar was rich and adorable, she didn't allow that to go to her head. Her kindness and sweet nature were apparent, and everyone who knew her loved her.

As Tamar entered adolescence, her body matured and her beauty blossomed. Her father's oldest son from a previous marriage began to take notice of her and his heart filled with lust. The more he fantasized about his young half sister, the more he longed for her. He hoped to get her alone, but he needed some bait to entice her. With the help of a friend, Tamar's half brother hatched an evil plan.

One day Tamar's half brother feigned illness and asked his father to send Tamar over to console him. Knowing Tamar's kindness, he requested that she personally make something he could eat. Tamar gladly went to help her sick half brother. She kneaded and baked his favorite bread, but that didn't satisfy him. He pleaded with her to come to his bedroom so that he could eat it from her own hand. Tamar loved him and wanted to do whatever she could to help him feel better. Little did she realize that when she took the bread to his room, the trap was about to snap. Once her half brother isolated her, he had no intention of eating, nor was he sick. Tamar pleaded with him to come to his senses and to stop, but her strength was no match for a grown man. He cruelly violated her, and when he was finished, he threw her out of his bedroom.

Devastated, she fled sobbing uncontrollably. Once home, her other brother took one look at her face and the disarray of her clothes and guessed what had happened. He made a feeble attempt to console Tamar by telling her not to let it bother her, but minimizing trauma never makes it better. When her father heard what had happened, he was furious but, for some unknown reason, did nothing. Tamar felt betrayed not only by her half brother, but also by her father, who could have brought justice to her but chose not to.

Perhaps you're thinking that Tamar is a client of mine. She is not, although much of what Tamar experienced has been experienced by many depressed women I have worked with. Tamar's story comes straight from the Bible (see 2 Samuel 13). Incest, rape, and child abuse are nothing new. These traumatic experiences are real and have life-changing implications for how children grow up.

Tamar lived the rest of her life in her brother's house, no longer a cheerful, vibrant young girl, but a desolate woman.

When Our Past Affects the Present

Research on depression and women shows a strong link between a traumatic childhood and the victim's future vulnerability to depression, as well as to numerous interpersonal difficulties. When children experience abusive trauma, whether physically, sexually, or emotionally, something dreadful and potentially life altering happens to them. In her book *Trauma and Recovery,* Judith Herman says,

> The emotional state of the chronically abused child ranges from a baseline of unease, through intermediate states of anxiety and dysphoria [Psychiatrists call dysphoria a dreadful feeling. It is a state of confusion, agitation, emptiness, and utter aloneness.], to extremes of panic, fury, and despair. Not surprisingly, a great many survivors develop chronic anxiety and depression which persist into adult life.[1]

Some Christians naively try to refute this reality. They say, "Forget the past" or "That was then, this is now" and wonder why some women just can't get over it and move on. Jesus knew better. Listen to what he said:

> Whoever causes one of these little ones who believe in Me to sin, it would be better for him if a millstone were hung around his neck, and he were drowned in the depth of the sea. Woe to the world because of offenses! For offenses must come, but woe to that man by whom the offense comes! (Matthew 18:6-7 NKJV).

Jesus knows wicked people victimize others. Because Satan is the prince of this world, he is always behind this kind of evil. Jesus sternly warns those who hurt children that they will receive the severest judgment, but what are the offenses that Jesus is talking about here?

The Greek word for "offenses" is *skándalon,* which means:

> The trigger in the trap on which the bait is placed and that springs the trap when it is touched by the animal, causing the trap to close. *Skándalon* always denotes the enticement or occasion leading to conduct which brings with it the ruin of the person in question.[2]

Jesus says when someone traps or entices a child and harms him or her, it profoundly affects that child's life. When a mouse grabs the cheese in a mousetrap and the trigger snaps, the mouse's future is forever changed. The mouse wasn't bad for wanting the cheese; that's normal behavior for mice. Tamar wasn't wrong for helping or loving her half brother. That is how God designed families to live. But sometimes when children seek familial love or attention, they get violated instead. Jesus knows that those who abuse children cause havoc with the children's view of themselves, their view of God, and their future ability to form trusting and loving relationships.

Here are the very personal words of women as they share about their past:

> When I was around 11, I was sexually abused, and this continued for many years. When I brought this to my mother's attention, she said my father would talk to him, but nothing ever changed. I feel this was a lot of the cause of my depression and drinking.   ~Kim

> My sister sexually experimented with me when she was 13 and I was eight years old. My parents never knew about it. I was extremely ashamed and guilty.
>   ~Janet

> I was sexually abused as a child with four different abusers, and that spilled over into two more as a young adult. I cannot change the past, but I can change the future by my choices now.   ~Laura

> I think the thing that caused my depression initially was sexual abuse as a child. Then professional sexual abuse sent me in a fast, downward spiral to a depth of despair I never would have believed could have existed.
>   ~Edie

I was involved in a sexual relationship with a 60-year-old man from the ages of 10 to 12 years old. Whether my parents knew or didn't know, they never said a word about it. It was never mentioned, never spoken of, nobody knew. As a teenager, I was suicidal. Nobody knew as I didn't tell anyone. My parents would complain that I was moody, but they never did anything.

~Jan

My sisters and I were sexually abused, as well as physically and emotionally abused. We also watched as my dad physically abused my mom on a regular basis. Violence and verbal abuse were the norm. Then there were times he was kind and nice. It was very confusing. My dad held us at gunpoint, and he threatened to kill me on more than one occasion. When I told my mom about the sexual abuse, she did not believe me. I was not allowed to have friends or play with the other children in the neighborhood. A close friend of my mom's also molested me. She didn't believe me when I told her about that either. Childhood abuse formed wrong thinking patterns. My family chose to ignore it and not talk about it until my sister was hospitalized. After we left my dad, the unspoken understanding was, "Don't talk about it and don't tell." I always felt trapped and powerless to change things.   ~Cindy

When a child's tender heart is betrayed in such a violent way, she is overwhelmed with the emotions of sorrow, rage, helplessness, confusion, and fear. Depending upon the age of the child, she often doesn't know how to cognitively process what is happening to her. Psychiatrist Judith Herman wrote:

Self-blame is congruent with the normal forms of thought of early childhood, in which the self is taken as

the reference point for all events. It is congruent with the
thought processes of traumatized people of all ages, who
search for faults in their own behavior in an effort to
make sense out of what has happened to them.[3]

It is beyond the scope of this book to look at all the issues that
confront someone dealing with sexual abuse in her past. An excellent book on this topic is called *On the Threshold of Hope* by Diane
Langberg. Please understand and accept that if you have experienced
sexual abuse in your childhood, you may have a harder battle than
others have in fighting depression. Because your body stayed on high
alert for many years, you may not know how to calm yourself in
healthy ways. You may not only need some medication to help you,
but you may also need to take it for a longer period of time than
women who have not experienced chronic abuse or other childhood
trauma. It is usually very helpful to spend some time working on these
hurts with a Christian counselor. God understands all these things
about you and your past. Please be gentle with yourself in the process
of healing. "He will not crush those who are weak or quench the
smallest hope. He will bring full justice to all who have been wronged"
(Isaiah 42:3 NLT).

Finding Freedom from the Past

Generally, it is not a good idea to continually rehash and rehearse
the past, though doing so with a Christian counselor may help you
gain a better understanding of the links between what happened to
you in the past and your current circumstances and choices. But
focusing your energy on examining your past will not necessarily help
you learn to live more productively or positively in the present. Good
counseling may encompass both elements, but there should always
be an emphasis on how to live better now.

Even if we have not been traumatized in our childhood, we all
have a past which establishes lifestyle patterns, good and bad, godly
and ungodly. These lifestyle patterns are the things that we must begin

to pay attention to so that we can learn to respond to our past differently.

As the sun sets, each day slips from the present and becomes the past. For many women, the pain of the past is more fresh and recent. Suffering and heartache are not from childhood events but from last week or last year, but they can't let it go and move beyond it. Sometimes their anguish isn't because of what someone has done to them, but because of what they have done to themselves or to someone they love (for example, aborting a baby). Every past mistake, sinful action, wrong word, and poor choice is rehearsed again and again as a means of reminding themselves what a failure they really are.

Whether the pain you're stuck in is from your recent past or from your childhood, from your own mistakes or from the sins of another, practicing these five steps will help you break free.

1. Acknowledge the Truth of What Happened

You can't move beyond something if you don't honestly face it. Whether it is your own past failures and mistakes or the sins of someone else, you can't fix or forgive something that "didn't happen," is "no big deal," "not really a problem," or "someone else's fault." These defenses are called denial, minimization, rationalization, and blame shifting, and they hinder you from facing the situation, feeling your emotions, and getting better.

Sometimes we don't know all the facts of what happened to us in our past. We have our perception of what happened and our feelings about it, but we are fuzzy on all of the details, especially when offenses occurred during our childhood. Acknowledging the truth of what happened to you doesn't mean you accurately recall every detail, but that you name it for what it is. For example, if you were violated or manipulated for sexual favors, then it wasn't love, it wasn't a mistake, it wasn't God's will, it wasn't your fault, and it wasn't because you were so cute and irresistible. It was sin.

Candace came to see me because she was depressed. In the process of getting to know her, I asked about her childhood. Her dad was an alcoholic and her mom worked hard to support the family. In spite of these hardships, Candace excelled at school and had many friends and outside activities. During the course of our sessions, she casually mentioned that when she was 13 years old, she had a two-year sexual relationship with a high school teacher. Now that she was a Christian, she felt guilty because he was married. Candace was not, however, able to see a connection with what happened back then and her current difficulties with men or depression.

Candace demonstrated a pattern of minimizing her problems and not facing the truth about events in her life. In this case, her teacher was a 35-year-old married man who should not have been flattering and preying on vulnerable pretty young students. As Candace began to recognize the true nature of their relationship, she not only felt guilty, but enraged. Feeling her anger and guilt was a necessary and important part of healing and breaking free, but she could only do that when she acknowledged this relationship for what it was.

Sometimes we do not want to face the truth about what others or we have done because we don't want to feel the strong emotions that accompany admitting that reality. We're afraid we won't be able to handle those feelings, so it's easier to shut down and turn off. This decision only makes matters worse and harder for you in the long run. As we have noted, the eventual consequence of choosing to handle your strong emotions this way is often depression.

When it is your own faults or failures that keep you bound to the past, rather than those of others, you must look truthfully at yourself. Often I find that a woman who rehearses and bemoans all her past mistakes, sins, and failures has difficulty accepting the truth that she sins and is not perfect. Her mourning is not because she's hurt another person or even offended God, but because she has disappointed herself. She cannot get over that she didn't handle something as perfectly as she would have liked and consequently hates herself. Instead of learning from her failures or confessing her sin and turning toward God for help to grow, she is always looking backward, beating herself up because she failed to live up to her own ideal standards. Perhaps as Gary Thomas writes, she has made an "idol out of her own piety."[4] French mystic Francois Fenelon encourages those of us who have this tendency with these wise words: "Go forward with confidence, without letting yourself be touched by the grief of a sensitive pride which cannot bear to see itself imperfect."[5]

2. Allow Yourself to Feel Your Feelings

By now I hope you are becoming alive to your deadened emotions, especially the ones you have not been willing to acknowledge in yourself. If you're starting to feel emotions, especially anger, that is already a huge step. However, as we've already learned, our feelings can become quite powerful, and if we are in the habit of letting them run roughshod over our lives, they can be quite scary. Perhaps we've been afraid to feel what we do because of how we might react when we become emotionally charged. Rather than struggle through that turmoil, it's easier to become numb. Feeling something strongly, however, does not mean that you have to act upon those feelings. Remember, our feelings match our thoughts, and so when we now start to think truthfully about something that is horrible or evil or sad, we will feel the corresponding emotions.

When we feel strong emotions, we need to be careful and wise. Feeling strongly does not entitle us to be reactionary or retaliatory in our behavior. When Candace began to feel rage at the reality of how much her teacher had taken advantage of her naivete and youthful foolishness, she wanted to "march right over to his house, scream at him, and rip his heart out." Then she wanted to report him to the school district and tell his wife and kids. Some of these actions might later be necessary and right, but for the moment it was important that Candace felt her emotions and processed them without taking specific action that she might later regret, especially when she felt so furious. Rage is much like toxic waste. We need to contain it and figure out how to dissipate it without letting it spill out all around us, hurting others and ourselves in the process.

Journal writing is an excellent way to dump your toxic feelings. No one sees your journal but you and God, and you are free to write down everything and anything you feel. I hope you have already been practicing this from the start of reading this book. If not, start now because you must allow yourself to express in a safe way what you feel. The process of writing helps you to release negative emotions from your body and your mind so that you can take the next step.

Another good way to release your feelings is to vent them with a trusted friend or counselor. You want someone who will accept that you are feeling strong negative emotions without scolding you, trying to fix you, or attempting to get you to stop feeling them. One word of caution I offer is that, once started, some women get stuck in this step. They don't move beyond expressing their feelings, venting them over and over, rehearsing every wrong ever done to them or by them, and by doing so, continue to be bound to their past, drowning in their own cesspool of hurt, self-pity, bitterness, rage, and helplessness. After feeling and verbalizing your negative emotions, let them go. You must now use your emotional energy to take the next step—and the next step—and the next step.

To get better you must move yourself forward, even when it is hard. If you find yourself unable to do this or are afraid of your strong emotions and feeling unsafe, please call a Christian counselor who will help you. Often it is unwise to do this work without professional guidance.

3. Release the Things You Are Not Responsible For

In the tangled web of sin, there are things we have done and things that have been done to us. Often we neglect to take responsibility for things we are responsible for or, conversely, take responsibility for things that are not our fault. Let me give you an example.

Andrea's father molested her when she was nine. The crackle of lightning and the crashing boom of thunder jolted her upright. Frightened, she scrambled into her parents' bed for comfort and protection, forgetting that her mom was in the hospital recuperating from surgery. She snuggled up next to her dad to feel safe. The next thing she remembers is his drunken breath all over her. Years later, even though a part of her knew better, Andrea still blamed herself. She told herself that if only she hadn't crawled into daddy's bed that night, it wouldn't have happened.

As we worked together, Andrea took the first step and emotionally faced the truth of what happened to her. The truth was that she wanted her dad to comfort and protect her, not to be sexual with her. He misused the situation and exploited it for his own selfish purposes. When Andrea acknowledged emotionally how her father sinfully used her, she felt flooded with hurt, confusion, anger, and deep, deep sadness. As she expressed and worked through these strong emotions, she finally let go of the responsibility she assumed for what happened that stormy night. It was not her fault that her father molested her. It was her dad's responsibility to act like a good father, even in tempting situations. She was a frightened little girl and acted appropriately for her age.

But Andrea's work in her quest to become free from the bondage of her past wasn't quite over yet. Andrea is no longer a little girl; she is an adult and needs to learn how to live as a mature one. Andrea must take responsibility for how she uses the excuse of what happened to her to continue to act helpless, refuse to try new things, and avoid owning the problems she creates by her passivity in relationships (for example, continued sexual exploitation in dating relationships). Without doing this important work, Andrea will stay stuck blaming her past for her current problems in living.

4. Take Responsibility for What You Can Change

You can't alter what happened to you, and you can't change other people into what you want (or wish) them to be. The only person you can change is yourself. As you work to do this, the changes you make impact the way your life goes in the present as well as in your future. Let's look at three things you can change about yourself that will help you break free from your past.

a. You can change the way you see yourself. We have already looked at the way you see yourself when we looked at self-image and self-esteem. Those who have been victimized and abused as children usually grow up with a grossly distorted picture of themselves and, sadly, have often made their victimization their identity instead of something that happened to them. To change this, know that you will need to invest some time and mental energy in revising your picture of yourself. The truest thing about you is what God says about you, not what you have been told, or even what you think. Here are some changes you might need to make:

What I Believe About Myself	What God Says
I'm a victim of my past.	I am not a victim anymore. God tells me I am more than a conqueror because he loves me so deeply (Romans 8:37).
I am helpless to change.	I can do all things through Christ who strengthens me (Philippians 4:13).
My life is ruined.	With God's power, he is able to transform any situation into something that is used for my good, his glory, and for his purposes (Romans 8:28). With God, all things are possible (Matthew 19:26; Mark 9:23).
I am damaged goods.	I am a new creation in Christ (2 Corinthians 5:17).

I am all alone.	I am never alone. God is always with me (Deuteronomy 31:6; Hebrews 13:5).
I have no family.	Even if my parents don't love me, God does (Psalm 27:10). I am adopted into his family and am his daughter (Ephesians 1:4-5; 1 John 3:1). He gives me friends and the body of Christ to encourage and support me (Ephesians 2:19).
I have no purpose.	I was created for a purpose before the world was made and God will fulfill it in me if I allow him to (Ephesians 2:10).

As we've discussed before, the way we think is strongly linked to how we feel. If we are thinking negative and untrue thoughts about ourselves, our emotions will follow suit and we will feel shame and depressed feelings. Part of taking responsibility now is for you to make the effort to see yourself truthfully. Practice rehearsing these crucial truths every day so that they might become more real to you (Philippians 4:8-9).

b. You can change the way you think about your past and the meaning you give it. As Christians we are all in the process of learning how to "take captive every thought to make it obedient to Christ" (2 Corinthians 10:5), as well as how to think about things from God's point of view instead of a worldly point of view (Romans 12:2; 2 Corinthians 5:16). We can't escape our history, but we can look at it differently.

Joseph is a perfect example of a man who had every reason to allow past events to destroy his present and future life. He was betrayed by his brothers and sold into slavery. Then he was falsely accused of attempted rape and unjustly thrown into prison, where he languished for years. I'm sure Joseph was tempted to feel sorry for himself and to become bitter toward God for permitting people to mistreat him, yet he did not. Joseph squarely faced the truth of what happened to him and vented his powerful emotions (see Genesis 45:2). He didn't blame himself for what his brothers did to him, but he did take responsibility for his own thoughts about it. He continuously submitted his life to God, and we hear him explain this to his brothers when he said, "Don't you see, you planned evil against me but God used those same plans for my good, as you see all around you right now—life for many people" (Genesis 50:20 MSG).

During a counseling session Francis felt extremely despondent over her past. Years earlier, she had played fast and loose. Drinking, doing drugs, and indulging in indiscriminate sexual relationships ruled her life. After coming to Christ, Francis felt forgiven, but she continued to see herself as damaged goods. She told herself that because of past immorality she was of no use to God and that she had no purpose. But that isn't true. For example, God used a former prostitute as part of Christ's genealogy, and one of the very first evangelists was a woman with a checkered past. In fact, it was because of the Samaritan woman's past that the people who knew her listened so intently (see Matthew 1:5 and Joshua 2 for the story of the prostitute, Rahab, and the story of the Samaritan woman as told in John 4).

God always uses broken, damaged, and sinful people to do all of his important work because we have all sinned and fallen short (Romans 3:23). As you learn to see your past differently, begin to look for strengths that have developed in you, not in spite of, but because of what happened to you. Ask God to show you specific ways he can use your past for his glory and to serve others. Don't allow Satan to warp your thoughts about how to think about yourself or what's happened to you. Satan tried to ruin your life in the past. Don't give him any ground in the present or the ability to rob you of your future.

c. You can change the way you respond to what happened in your past and what happens in your present. Not everyone who grows up in an abusive family becomes an abuser or a continuous victim of abuse. Not everyone who is treated poorly stays stuck in self-pity, bitterness, hate, or an unforgiving spirit. Not everyone who is sinned against shuts off her emotions or retaliates. The temptation to respond in unhealthy, hurtful, or sinful ways when sinned against by someone is universal, but God gives us other choices.

Even when nothing hurtful or sinful is happening to us, we all respond in our own unique ways to our environment. For example, when a mom tells her children, "No, you may not have a cookie," one child walks away mumbling under her breath, another throws a temper tantrum, and a third says, "Okay, Mom." Why is this? Jesus tells us why. He says that out of the overflow of our heart our mouth speaks (Luke 6:45). What comes out of our mouth when life happens reveals what is in our heart—good or bad, right or wrong, sinful or pure. Understanding this truth is important so that we don't blame other people for our responses. The child who threw a temper tantrum might blame her mother, saying, "It is your fault I acted this way because you wouldn't give me a cookie." We laugh, but those of us who are moms often use the same excuse when we tell our children, "It's all your fault I screamed at you because you wouldn't listen."

It's true that people provoke us or hurt us, and this tempts us to sin, but how we respond to what they do or don't do comes from our heart; our responses are our own choices. Over time these choices become our preferred patterns and solidify into habits. These habits become so automatic we don't recognize them anymore as our choice and usually blame others for the way we respond, saying, "You made me so mad." But if we want to learn to handle things differently from now on, we must take responsibility for our feelings, our thoughts, and our reactions in each and every circumstance.

Our lifestyle patterns and interpersonal styles are definitely influenced by what happens to us, but more than that, they are shaped by what we do with what happens to us. Many people fail to grow during adversity or learn to handle problems in life constructively because they forget this important truth. Instead, they live as if they are merely victims of life's difficulties, continually blaming others for the way they are.

Remember, you may not be able to control what happens to you, but you can always choose how you respond to it. The apostle Paul reminds us of this choice when he writes, "Don't let evil get the best of you; get the best of evil by doing good" (Romans 12:21 MSG).

5. Work Toward Forgiveness

Finally, to move beyond your past, decide in your heart to work toward forgiving those who have hurt you or sinned against you. God's Word never lies, and it is always the best resource on how to live in an emotionally healthy way. Jesus tells us to forgive others when they mistreat or hurt us. "How many times?" Peter asks. "Don't count," Jesus responds (Matthew 18:21-22).

The apostle Paul also encourages us to not let the sun go down while we are still angry, for this gives the devil a foothold into our heart (Ephesians 4:26-27). The Bible tells us to "get rid of all bitterness, rage, anger, harsh words, and slander, as well as all types of malicious behavior. Instead, be kind to each other, tenderhearted, forgiving one another, just as God through Christ has forgiven you" (Ephesians 4:31-32 NLT).

I find that many women I've worked with either forgive too quickly, before doing the emotional work they need to in order to process and get rid of their hurt and anger, or they don't forgive at all because they have erected large, thick walls of bitterness and resentment.

Jesus tells us to forgive one another, and that alone is a good enough reason to do it, but forgiveness is a good thing to do even for those who don't know Jesus or believe in him. Long before modern medicine studied the physiological effects of chronic anger, resentment, and bitterness on the body, God knew that harboring these toxic emotions could not only damage our health but also ruin our lives. He warns us to get rid of them promptly.

God knows sin destroys us. It is not the sin that is committed against us that wields the fatal blow. Rather, it is our own sinful reaction to the things that have happened to us. Unresolved anger often turns to depression, self-pity, bitterness, and resentment, and these things poison our body and our soul. A person finds healing through the process of forgiveness, both receiving forgiveness and extending forgiveness. That is why God is so insistent that we forgive. He doesn't want sin to ruin our lives.

Please don't misunderstand what forgiveness is. Forgiveness isn't excusing the offender or minimizing their offense. Forgiveness is your decision to cancel the debt they rightfully owe you. Many protest here and become stuck because they are rightly deserving of justice or an apology or some restitution for the offenses done to them. They don't want to cancel the debt owed because it feels so unfair to them. Yet if they are waiting for the person to repent or apologize or show remorse, they may wait a very long time.

In the Old Testament story, Joseph forgave his brothers for selling him into slavery. Joseph's obedience freed him to be used by God in Egypt. But Joseph never initiated reconciliation with his betrayers—nor did he expose himself to them when he first saw them again. Why? He did not trust them. He was kind and gracious to them because he forgave them, but he tested them to see if they had repented and changed their jealous and self-centered ways. Joseph invited them back into relationship with him after they passed the test (see Genesis 42–46). Joseph's forgiveness and his brothers' repentance were both necessary to bring reconciliation *and* restoration to their relationship.

For some of you, you may never see repentance from the person who hurt you. Sandy lived stuck in her past, angry that her father abused her. She refused to give up her anger until "he admits what he did and says he's sorry." When she confronted him and asked for an apology, he told her she was crazy and denied everything she accused him of doing. That left her waiting for something that may never happen. She allowed her father to continue to ruin her present and her future because he would not do what she longed for him to do. Sandy's anger and lack of forgiveness wasn't hurting Sandy's father. He lived selfishly just as he always did. It was Sandy's life that was hurt by her angry and bitter heart. Finally forgiving her father released Sandy from those toxic emotions. Her father will still have to give an account for what he did to Sandy, only it will be God, not Sandy who will judge him.

In my own life, forgiveness usually comes in steps and cycles. It is not a one-time, over-and-done-with event. First, I decide to forgive, exercising my will. Then I begin the process of letting go, releasing the anger, the hurt, and my desire to retaliate. I appeal to God for justice and turn the situation over to him. I also ask him to help me see my offender and myself differently. This is very helpful. When God shows me my own sinful nature and the things I am capable of doing, then I can have some genuine compassion on my offender because, but for God's grace, I may have done the same thing. I no longer want to see my offender only as someone who did something wrong, but also as someone who has done some things right. I no longer want to see him or her as a victimizer, but as a person with weaknesses of character and a sinful heart, just like me.

When hurtful memories surface and I'm tempted to dwell on the wrongs done to me, I continue this process and keep at it until the negative emotions and thoughts are no longer in the front of my mind. They are fading and moving to the past, right where they belong.

To practice forgiveness, walk regularly through these four steps: Decide—Begin—Continue—Keep at it. As we do this, we are changing. We are no longer defining ourselves by what has happened to us, but we are instead seeing ourselves by what God is doing in us. Our healing becomes a powerful conduit for God's love and grace to flow to others, and we can honestly say what Satan meant for evil, God is using for good.

Moving Forward by Exercising Your Will

Something to Think About

As we have seen, moving from the past to living in the present involves your whole heart. You will need to feel your emotions, venting them in a safe way and allowing their intensity to diminish. You will need to challenge your thinking with the truth by identifying the lies you have believed and perhaps even hidden behind. But these things are only accomplished with the gentle or sometimes firm prodding of your will. You will not do these things automatically. You will need to choose to, not because I tell you to, but because you know it is important and necessary to your well-being, even if you don't feel like it.

Oftentimes when we exercise our will in this manner, we feel like a hypocrite. This is because we've been taught that if we don't feel something, there is no genuineness to the actions. But this is not true. Remember, our feelings aren't the only things to consider in determining the authenticity of our decisions. Our will and our thoughts also play an important role in who we are. Jesus didn't feel like going to the cross. His will and his thoughts made that decision. But that decision was made because he wanted to please God with all his heart, not because someone made him do it.

Choosing to release the past and forgive, even when your emotions are reluctant, isn't hypocrisy; it's obedience.

Something to Do

Pick one event from your past that you have not let go of. Perhaps it is a childhood wound or rejection. Maybe it is something someone has done that hurt you more recently. It might even be something you have done to yourself. If you're reluctant, ask God to help you have the courage to get started.

Choose the first thing you'd like to release and begin by naming it. Work through the five steps I've given you in this chapter, writing down as you go all your thoughts and feelings about it.

1. Acknowledge the truth of what happened.

2. Allow yourself to feel your feelings.

3. Release the things you are not responsible for.

4. Take responsibility for what you can change.

5. Work toward forgiveness.

Ask God to change your thinking so that you will know how to think truthfully about your situation. Invite him to help you change your perspective on your past and, the way Joseph did, help you see things through an eternal lens. When you struggle, confess your doubts and pray for more faith to believe God and what he tells you instead of your own thoughts and feelings. Seek to learn how to respond to hurts and wrongs with truth and grace so that you will know how to not be overcome by evil but to overcome evil with good. When you're reluctant to let go and forgive, ask God to give you the willingness to forgive, not because you have to, but because you want to please and obey him.

Repeat these steps with each painful past offense until you feel that your past is no longer ruling your present. Here is a sample prayer you may want to pray.

> Dear Jesus,
>
> Help me to be free from the bondage of my past. I no longer want to live like a victim. I want to live like a daughter of the King. I no longer want to hide from the truth of what happened to me, but I don't want to be embittered by it, either. Teach me to see things from your

perspective so that I am neither hindered by my sin or the sin of others against me. Set my heart free so that I may fully live in the present, glorify you, and find my life in you.

I see how important it is that I let go of these things. Help me take responsibility for what I need to do to make progress in this area. Help me forgive those who have hurt me. When I doubt, give me faith. When I'm unwilling, give me the desire to be made willing. Amen.

How do you know you're finished with your past? A good marker is when you are no longer waiting for anything. You're not waiting for an apology. You're not waiting for anyone to fall on his or her face and ask for your forgiveness. You're not waiting for your parents or former husband or anyone else who has hurt you to finally see the light and give you their love or approval.

You are free when you are looking more upward and outward instead of inward and backward. You are free when you are starting to love and are not shutting down your emotions or allowing your heart to be filled with anger and resentment. You have moved on and are living and creating your present story with your past as your background, not your foreground.

I Feel All Alone

If one falls down, his friend can help him up.
But pity the man who falls
and has no one to help him up!
Also, if two lie down together,
they will keep warm.
But how can one keep warm alone?
ECCLESIASTES 4:10-11

What a man desires is unfailing love.
PROVERBS 19:22

Painful relationships in our past aren't the only source of significant distress we experience. Present relationship difficulties and sinful relational styles make a woman more vulnerable to depression. The arrows that pierce the deepest come from those we love and hope will not hurt us. Psychologist Richard O'Connor in his book *Undoing Depression* says, "Depression is both caused by and a cause of poorly functioning relationships."[1] The National Institute of Mental Health (NIMH) indicates that the highest rates for depression for both men and women are among those who are separated and divorced.

The condition of a marital relationship is a significant factor in predicting depression, especially in women. The NIMH reports, "Lack of an intimate, confiding relationship, as well as overt marital disputes, have been shown to be related to depression in women. In fact, rates of depression were shown to be highest among unhappily married women."[2]

Feelings of loneliness are not always subdued by living with a family or attending a church full of people. A depressed woman feels as though she is standing behind a glass wall or wrapped in a dark cloud. When her depression is severe, there is no interest in people or energy to connect and be involved with others. At times, even conversation feels too difficult for her. More than ever a depressed woman needs loving people in her life, but she often feels ashamed over her depression and withdraws from her friends and loved ones.

> *Because of my depression I have lost a few friends, but I have come to the conclusion that these friendships were not real or true friendships. When I have a bad day, I still find myself shutting people out or lashing out.*
>
> *~ Pam*

> *My relationships have been strained due to my depression. My husband is trying to understand me and my children are concerned. I've separated myself from some of my friends because I don't have the energy to listen to their problems and be a friend to them.   ~ Alice*

> *My relationships with others definitely worsened because I was broken and no one understood my fragile condition. I began isolating myself from everyone.   ~Stacy*

No One Understands

Friends and family members often don't know what to do to help a depressed woman feel better and sometimes become impatient and frustrated trying. They may offer advice like "Just get over it" or "Pick yourself up by your bootstraps" or "Try to look at the bright side of things," which sound trite and offer no real solutions to a depressed woman's plight. If those things helped, she would have already done them. Others scold or spiritualize. They say, "You're just feeling sorry for yourself" or "If you would trust God more, you'd feel better." Although there may be some truth to what they say at times, com ments of this kind usually make a depressed woman feel even more guilty. Depression isn't that simple. There are plenty of people who don't trust God and feel sorry for themselves yet don't get depressed, and many others who deeply trust God and still get depressed.

Depression is a lonely experience, but as you read the words of the other women throughout this book, I want you to know *you are not alone.* The ache in your soul can be helped, but you need loving connections with God and with others to heal. It's hard, but instead of withdrawing, reach out. Allow others to love you and help you.

Starting on page 240 is a sample letter you may want to give your loved ones to help them understand depression and what you need from them. Whatever you say to them, it is important to have the love, support, and understanding of the people around you as you go through this difficult experience.

Does Anyone Care?

A woman who regularly experiences indifference, contempt, abuse, scorn, and rejection in her relationships is a prime candidate for depression. She tells herself that no one cares for her. No one wants to listen or know her deeply. She does not feel valued and impor- tant based on who she is, but instead is only wanted for what she gives to others in whatever way they require. She rarely feels any rec- iprocity in her relationships.

If married, she longs for connection and companionship, but instead of the intimacy she craves, she experiences apathy, disrespect, or sometimes physical abuse. She feels as though she's dying inside, but she's convinced she is powerless to change anything. Over time, withdrawing seems like the only way to endure the pain and con- tain the anger she feels. Eventually depression may take over.

Listen once again to the words of women who struggled with depression and problems in their relationships:

My bad marriage and not being able to know what were lies versus truth led me to withdraw and become depressed. Once I withdrew from one person I didn't feel I could open up to others and gradually withdrew from many people. By that time I was so self-absorbed that I felt no one cared.   ~Sue

When I am rejected, I struggle with the urge to get depressed.   ~Anna

Before I knew Christ, I believed my value as a person was based totally on my performance. The focus of my life was to please other people, no matter what. For some reason, people in my life placed unrealistic expectations on me. When I failed to meet their expectations, very often their responses were hurtful and demeaning. I began to feel rejected, and I felt like a failure. I was so desperate for approval and acceptance, I reached the point of compromising myself and my beliefs. I made a lot of poor and unwise decisions. As a result, I didn't like myself or my life.   ~Deb

I've finally understood that the driving force in my life has been my idolatrous desire for love and acceptance. When I haven't gotten what I've craved from my husband or others I want to love and accept me, I have gotten depressed.   ~Gwen

I do not know how to love or how to be loved. I desperately desire intimacy, but I run away from it at the same time. So I'm not sure which came first, my depression or poor relationships. I think my husband has been on the receiving end of the effects of my depression, but in my depression I also sought out relationships that would fuel my low self-esteem. I have some very close women friends,

whom I am extremely grateful for, but there is really
no one who really knows the desires of my heart or the
struggles except God, and, sadly, I keep pushing God out.

~ Sarah

What's Wrong?

God designed human beings to live in companionship, harmony, and love, first with him but also with one another. Adam and Eve experienced this perfect unity and intimate fellowship. Trust, intimacy, companionship, and happiness all flourished in the garden of Eden, but Eve's decision to believe the serpent instead of what God told her and Adam's decision to follow Eve changed everything. As a result, sin entered all human relationships. Instead of comfort and security, now there was shame and fear. There was no longer intimacy, peace, and unity, but disconnection, tension, and turmoil. Nothing would ever be the same. As time passed, Adam and Eve's children didn't know God's love the way their parents had. Instead of experiencing mutually loving relationships with God's love as the source, selfishness, shame, envy, fear, and pride now ruled.

Things haven't changed over the years. Sin, both our own sin and the sin of others, robs us from experiencing the kind of relationship with God and with others that God intended. Without a secure foundation in God's love, we search for human love to fill us up and make us feel valuable and worthwhile. This strategy always fails because human love was never designed to totally fulfill us and make us happy. No one will ever understand us and care for us as much as we want. Only God's love is that good and his understanding that complete. Even the best human love is laced with finite limitations and sin.

When our human relationships become disappointing or are in conflict, God shows us through his Word what we must do to facilitate healing and reconciliation. However, instead of deepening our intimacy with him and allowing him to teach us how to form and maintain loving relationships, we too often continue to try to make things work on our own or we give up and slide into despair and depression.

Overcoming Aloneness: Creating and Enjoying Godly Relationships

Fellowship and intimacy are absolutely essential to our well-being, growth, and maturity. The longing for love, connection, and relationship is tightly woven into our human fabric. In fact, we won't fully develop as human beings without loving interactions with other people. An infant that is physically cared for but emotionally and relationally neglected will fail to thrive and may die.

Christians know that God designed us for intimate connection with him and with one another, but we also know that not all of our relationships are functioning the way God intended them to. I have worked with people in relationships that could only be described as miserable, hateful, and abusive. No matter how comfortable their external circumstances were, individuals in these relationships experienced constant inner conflict and stress.

On the other hand, I have also observed relationships that were not perfect but in which there was mutual love, safety, and respect. People in these relationships displayed resilience against life's turmoil and were able to depend on one another during times of trouble. Loving relationships provide a tremendous sense of inner joy and well-being, even when our external lives become stressful. When we don't have good relationships, depression is common.

Life is excruciatingly painful when loss, stress, and physical afflictions ravish our spirit or body, but when a loving community surrounds you, it provides good insulation against depression. Psychiatrist Valerie Davis Raskin writes, "Women's vulnerability to and recovery from emotional illnesses naturally rests in a place of connection to others."[3] God knew that. That is why he designed the family and the church, the family of God, to be a place of deep and loving fellowship.

Because intimacy and connection with others is crucial to our emotional and spiritual health and maturity, it is vital that we understand what personal characteristics are necessary to achieve loving relationships and acquire the skills to maintain them. Jesus wisely warns us that a house built on sand will not stand for long. When the inevitable winds and storms howl, only a house built on a stable foundation will last.

Likewise, attempting connection and intimacy with someone without having a secure base is shaky. Because of sin, even good relationships can be difficult and involve heartache. That is why it is so crucial that we learn what attributes to look for in someone as well as develop them in ourselves, so that our closest relationships are based on commitment, honesty, and mutuality. When we have these three essential characteristics in place, trust, warmth, goodwill, and affection can flourish.

Commitment

To build good relationships with others, we must begin with ourselves. Christ calls us to love one another as he has loved us (John 15:12), but oftentimes we are more intent on looking for people to love us instead of learning how to love others as Jesus calls us to. When we do this, we end up with self-centered rather than God-centered relationships.

Sadly, today I find people unsure what biblical love looks like. To love others as Jesus did, we must start with an attitude of commitment. Often we think this means we must be committed to a relationship no matter what. That kind of thinking gets many women in trouble. The Bible never commands us to be unconditionally committed to a relationship. That could be dangerous, and it is unwise. Jesus himself did not pursue people who refused his conditions of relationship, yet he still loved them (see, for example, Christ's interaction with the rich young ruler in Mark 10:17-22).

Every relationship has conditions that must be met to facilitate trust and security. For example, when a couple agrees to marry, they make promises to each other to nurture and honor the integrity and purity of their marriage. If the promises are repeatedly and carelessly broken and there is no repentance and change, a loving relationship is impossible, even if the couple remains legally married.

We know that Jesus tells us to love one another. Christ even tells us to love our enemies, but, please hear this: *Jesus does not require us to have a relationship with our enemies.* The commitment we must have if we want God-centered relationships is a commitment to God that we will seek the other person's best. That gets confusing, because we can easily deceive ourselves into thinking we're showing love to someone, when in reality, even if well intentioned, we aren't.

For example, Shirley often stepped in and completed her child's homework assignments because he "forgot" to do them. Instead of allowing him to experience the natural consequences for his lack of responsibility (a poor grade), she sacrificially stayed up and did his assignments while he slept. Shirley also gave up going to college two evenings a week because her husband didn't want to watch the children.

Shirley may tell herself that her actions demonstrate a commitment to sacrificially love her son and husband no matter what, but the truth is her behavior wasn't motivated by love but by fear. Shirley was fearful that her son's teacher would think poorly of her if he came unprepared to class, so she completed his assignments. She also was afraid that her husband would be angry with her if she told him, "I don't like this arrangement. I'd like you to spend some time caring for our children in the evenings. Besides that, I want to complete college and this is the only way I can do it." Instead of speaking to him about her concerns, she dropped her classes and stayed home.

Shirley did not act in either her child's or husband's best interests. It's obvious in this example that it is in her child's long-term best interests to learn from his mistakes, and to remember to do his assignments in order to grasp what his teacher wanted him to learn through his homework. It is also clearly in her husband's best interests for him to learn how to be a good father and for her children to have quality time with their dad. As long as Shirley enables both to remain irresponsible and childish, they won't learn or grow.

When Shirley is committed to making everyone happy with her instead of loving them as God intended, her relationships will always grow more and more strained. Shirley's husband and son may enjoy the arrangement, but eventually Shirley will tire of it. It is not only in the best interests of her son and husband that Shirley learns how to love better, it is also in the long-term best interests of their relationships.

Sometimes doing what is in someone's best interests isn't so easily discernable. When this is the case, general biblical principles will help guide our actions. It is always good to encourage someone's positive qualities and look for ways to do so, even if it's difficult to find something commendable (Hebrews 10:24). It is always in someone's best interests to pray for them, even sacrificially through fasting or intercession for extended periods of time. The apostle Paul tells us that one of the characteristics of godly love is that it does no harm to a neighbor (Romans 13:10); therefore, we are careful with our tongue and our behaviors, even toward someone we don't like. We show respect toward someone, not because he or she is acting worthy of it, but because they are a fellow human being, created in the image of God, and we do not want to disrespect God's image in them (1 Peter 2:17; James 3:9-10).

God's Word also tells us that it is never in someone's best interest for us to make it easy for them to sin. That is bad for them and harmful to their relationship with God and with us. Therefore, we should *never* sacrifice ourselves in order to allow someone to continue to sin, whether sinning in general or sinning against us.

Many women are confused about what biblical love looks like in these instances. For example, Joan continued to permit her husband to live at home despite his drunken rages and abusive behavior because she said, "I love him and I'm praying he will change." Of course Joan prays her husband will change, but is it in his best interests or giving him an opportunity to change when she allows him to continue to sin with no consequences? Please hear this. The most loving thing you can do for someone who is out of control with sin is to allow the person to experience the consequences of his or her behavior. Proverbs 19:19 says, "A hot-tempered man must pay the penalty; if you rescue him, you will have to do it again." It is only when we experience the pain and ugliness of our sin that we are most open and receptive to God and to our need to repent and change our ways. Otherwise, it's easy to continue to deceive ourselves into believing that our sin is not that bad.

When we commit ourselves to love someone, we don't promise to look out for what's easiest for them, or necessarily for what they want us to do, but instead, we look for what God says is best for them. As we love them that way, they may even become angry with us, but that's what God's love looks like toward us. He always acts in our best interests, even though sometimes what's best doesn't feel comfortable to us at the moment. C.S. Lewis wisely puts it this way. He says, "Love is something more stern and splendid than mere kindness."[4]

It is much easier for most of us to keep quiet or walk away rather than to be honest about our feelings or experiences, even when the relationship is only professional or casual. However, in order for any relationship to be maintained or to flourish, honesty is absolutely essential.

Honesty

Without honesty, it is impossible to move a relationship toward intimacy and deeper trust. No relationship can mature without honest talk. Being honest with someone does not mean we take off all our emotional clothes, so to speak, just so someone knows everything about us. Not every relationship deserves or warrants that level of intimacy, especially if there is no mutual commitment to love. God ordained marriage as the primary human relationship where, ideally, we feel free to express ourselves most openly and honestly. However, because of the Fall, Adam and Eve covered up, hiding themselves from one another and from God. Coverings give us some protection for our vulnerabilities, and we can hide our flaws under them. One of the greatest joys in a relationship though, is to know and be known by another. If we regularly hide and protect ourselves from others, we rob ourselves of the comfort of being known and loved, warts and all.

Being truthful does not mean we are free to blurt out whatever we want without any reflection or prayer. God's Word cautions us against that kind of speech (Ephesians 4:25-32). We must learn to speak the truth, but only in love. Speaking a hard word to someone because they have hurt us does not mean it is a harsh word. Honest words may hurt, but they are structured to offer help and healing (see, for example, Psalm 141:5; Proverbs 27:6; Matthew 18:15-17; Galatians 6:1).

Harsh words attack, blame, and shame a person. They are used as a weapon, but the book of Proverbs teaches us that the "tongue of the wise brings healing" (Proverbs 12:18). Regular or frequent use of harsh words toward a person will destroy goodwill and warmth, killing intimacy and often destroying the relationship. In the next chapter we will look at how to handle conflict so that, when necessary, we will know how to use our commitment to love in combination with honest words to facilitate healing in a fractured relationship.

There is a kind of dishonesty I often see in women (especially those prone to depression), and it is lethal to intimacy and to your own emotional and spiritual health. It is called "pretending," and women do it all the time. We pretend something doesn't matter to us when it does matter. We pretend we want to do something when we don't. We act happy when we're hurting. We say something doesn't bother us when our blood is boiling. We pretend we're not as smart or talented or as resourceful as we are so we don't threaten a man's ego. We act as if we're more spiritual than we are so others will like us or look up to us. We become so good at pretending that we forget who we are and what we're passionate about. Instead, we morph ourselves into whatever we think others want us to be just so they will like us or want to be with us. In the process, we forfeit the joy of being known and accepted for who we are. Not only that, when we live for the love and approval of others, we lose out on becoming the woman God designed us to be.

If you recognize you are pretending and you want to get better, you must take responsibility for this tendency and stop. First, you must learn to speak the truth in your relationships, not because you feel like it, but because you are trying to make a change in order to facilitate deeper, more real relationships and are taking a step of obedience with God.

Perhaps you're thinking, *If I do that, I won't have any relationships. If I'm honest with who I am or how I feel, no one will like me or want to be with me.* That is probably not true, although you're terrified to test it to find out. If, for example, you say to your girlfriend, "No, I don't like pizza. I'd rather go out for Chinese food," are you thinking she'll reject you? If she is a real friend, it's not likely, even if she loves pizza.

What if you tell your mother, "No, we aren't coming over for Christmas this year. We need to establish some traditions in our own home, but you're welcome to come and spend the day with us." Do you think she'll disown you? More likely, she will be disappointed or surprised that you spoke out about your own desires, but eventually she will accept your feelings about the holidays and ideally compromise with you.

We fail to be honest because we tell ourselves that we can't bear to have anyone disappointed with us or unhappy with us, but the truth is, every relationship has disappointments, even good relationships. No one can ever do everything someone else might want or say they need all of the time. Even Jesus disappointed people, and he was perfect. He didn't heal everyone who wanted healing; he didn't do everything people wanted him to do. He loved people, but he wasn't controlled by his approval ratings. He did what he believed his Father was telling him to do and didn't allow other people's agendas to throw him off (see Mark 1:29-38 for an example of this). You need not feel guilty because you cannot be all things to all people. You need to accept the limitations of your humanity.

When we first stop pretending and start to speak honestly about who we are or what we can or can't do or what we want in our relationships, we always feel awkward and uncomfortable. Don't let those feelings stop you. Most people feel a little foolish when trying new things. Practice using your words for good. Stop placating someone with dishonest or insincere sentiment; rather, learn to speak the truth in love so that there is an opportunity for mutual caring and understanding to be expressed.

Some of you may be in relationships that are very lopsided. Perhaps you're afraid that if you stop pretending that you like this arrangement, the taker in the relationship won't hang around. You may be right. Your honest talk might also be just the impetus he or she needs to change and start learning how to give back and think of someone else for a while. That would be good for him or her, good for you, and good for your relationship. Likewise, if you have surrounded yourself with people who aren't used to you speaking the truth to them or saying no about things, your relationships may become more strained when you stop pretending. It helps if you explain to people the changes that you are trying to make. Usually when they understand why you're acting differently, they're more accepting. If that doesn't happen and there is continued resistance to your honest talk, know that without mutual caring, a genuine, loving relationship is impossible.

Mutuality

Whenever we express our true feelings, thoughts, and desires to someone, we open our heart and invite them to know us and to care about who we are and what we want. We do this superficially when we ask the waiter in the restaurant to put the salad dressing on the side, or when we tell him our food came out wrong and ask him to replace it. (Some of you may be cringing right now because you can't imagine yourself engaging in small doses of honest talk with strangers and directly asking for something.)

We also attempt to be known when we ask our husband, girl-friend, or parent to listen to our feelings or perspectives. We want them to care about an issue that is important to us or to share in our excitement about our dreams. When we are rebuffed or ignored, it hurts deeply.

The apostle Paul prayed that as believers we would be knit together by strong ties of love for one another (Colossians 2:2). This desire is not selfish or wrong; it is good and God given. Jesus longed for a deeper relationship with the people of Israel, but they were unwilling. They were receptive when he helped them, but they were not inter-ested in trusting him, believing him, or spending quality time with him. They wanted a one-sided relationship where Jesus gave and they received. Jesus wanted more and, most of the time, so do we (Matthew 23:37).

We all experience people in our life who never give anything in return, and we are still called to love them. They may even be mem-bers of our own family. Abigail's marriage was loveless and difficult, but it did not make her bitter or depressed. She did not fool herself about who her husband was and even took a courageous stand against him with King David to make the best of a difficult situa-tion (1 Samuel 25). The Bible describes her as an intelligent and beau-tiful woman.

Like Abigail, how can we be involved in difficult relationships without becoming depressed or resentful? The Scriptures tell us this kind of sacrificial love is possible when we know and rest in the reality that we are fully loved and completely understood by Almighty God (John 13:34; 1 John 4:16). When we know his love for us, we trust that he gives us everything we need for life and for godliness (Philippians 4:19; 2 Peter 1:3-4). Therefore, although we are hurt and disappointed when others fail to return our love or they reject us, we are neither depleted nor destroyed.

We desperately need to be filled with more of God's love. Then and only then are we empowered to love others well, whether or not they love us back or are even nice to us. However, please understand this important truth. We may initiate loving interactions with others, but this in no way qualifies as a loving relationship. Jesus gave to many people who never gave him anything in return *and* he enjoyed mutually caring relationships.

Sometimes I'm afraid that, as women, we confuse unconditional love with unconditional relationship.[5] We cannot expect good relationships with people where one or more of these sinful ways of relating predominates: superficiality, withdrawal, pretense, coldness, indifference, disrespect, and/or abuse. It's impossible. It *is* possible to interact with someone who is indifferent or disrespectful or even abusive in a respectful way and to love him or her as Christ calls us to, but there is no enjoyment or pleasure in this interaction. It is not a godly or healthy relationship. It is all hard work.[6] In the same manner, if we too are guilty of relating with others in these sinful ways, perhaps this is one reason why our relationships fail and we don't experience the close connections with others that we desire.

Commitment, honesty, and mutuality lay the foundation to building good relationships and result in warmth, trust, security, pleasure, and happiness. We enjoy being with the other person and they enjoy us. We feel heard and valued not only for what we do for him or her but for who we are. Intimacy deepens as we feel secure and safe with one another. Together we experience the blessings of being known and enjoyed, and we trust that the other person is for us and not against us. Without a commitment to love, honest conversation, and mutual care, positive emotions are minimal or absent, and usually negative emotions predominate and the relationship becomes strained.

Becoming More Honest in Relationships

Something to Think About

We all remember the nursery rhyme "Sugar and spice and everything nice, that's what little girls are made of." Many women are too nice, and it gets them in trouble. The dictionary defines nice as "socially agreeable and pleasant," the very thing that often hinders honesty in relationships. Interestingly, the Bible never tells us we must be nice. Rather, it encourages kindness toward one another (Ephesians 4:32). There is a huge difference. Kindness is defined as being "sympathetic, gracious, and considerate." To have healthy and mutually satisfying relationships, we must stop being so nice and learn to speak the truth in love, speaking sympathetically, graciously, and considerately as we share honestly about who we are, what we want, or how we feel.

Something to Do

If you recognize yourself in this chapter as a pretender, changing is a process and doesn't happen overnight. Sometimes it's easier to do what everyone else wants instead of learning to think for yourself and figure out what you want. Practice first at being honest with casual or professional relationships, such as with a store clerk, waitress, or your pharmacist. Ask this person for something you'd like and observe his or her reaction. If she appears irritated with your request, calmly smile and tell her that you appreciate her service and repeat what you'd like. If you become anxious, remind yourself that this is a practice session to learn how to build healthier relationships. Therefore, you must learn to tolerate the disapproval of others without backing down or pretending everything is fine. (And, if it becomes too unpleasant, you never have to go back to that store.)

Remember, the more you practice something, the easier it gets.

Working Through Conflict

Blessed are the peacemakers,
for they will be called sons of God.
MATTHEW 5:9

If it is possible, as far as it depends on you,
live at peace with everyone.
ROMANS 12:18

Fearing people is a dangerous trap,
but to trust the LORD means safety.
PROVERBS 29:25 NLT

Dana threw up her arms. "I don't know how to make them happy. Nothing I do is ever enough," she cried. "When I do what my husband wants, my mother gets mad. When I listen to my mom and do what she wants, then Ted's upset."

Dana came for counseling because of her depression, and it was obvious to me that much of her depression revolved around the stressful people in her life and her inner turmoil of trying to keep them happy with her. Dana couldn't say no or tolerate conflict without feeling guilty and anxious. She'd try to please her mother and Ted, but after a while she'd become frustrated and scream at them both, hating herself for her ugly outbursts. When the inner turmoil and outer conflicts with her mother and husband became too stressful, Dana shut down and grew more and more depressed.

Dana's climb out of depression involved learning to understand her people-pleasing tendencies and how to handle her feelings of anxiety, anger, and guilt when people in her life were unhappy with her. Dana also needed to learn how to biblically approach disagreements with Ted and her mother that occurred whenever she attempted to voice her own opinions and feelings on things or didn't want to do what they wanted her to.

Why Am I the Way I Am?

Before Dana could learn to speak more truthfully about her feelings or try to negotiate some of the conflicts between herself and others, she needed to better understand what was going on in her heart. Dana had the heart of a peacekeeper rather than a peacemaker. To achieve a semblance of peace, she avoided conflict without ever honestly discussing or resolving anything. Hot issues were routinely shoved under the rug.

Everything within Dana shrank at the thought of honest talk that might bring about the dreaded disapproval of others. She worried that if she disagreed with her husband, he'd get mad and not speak to her. She feared standing up to her mom because she felt guilty for disappointing her. Even when she knew what God wanted from her, Dana rarely moved forward without the approval of the significant people in her life. If they showed disappointment or disapproval, Dana quickly backed down.

When Dana's mother announced she was taking Dana's young daughter to Florida for a week's vacation, Dana acquiesced to her mother's wishes knowing this decision would upset Ted. Whenever Ted overspent their credit card limit without telling her, she became angry and blew up at him, though they never seriously talked about the issue or sought a solution to Ted's spending habits.

The problem Dana had was deeper than her inability to say no or set appropriate boundaries with people. Even if I taught her those skills, without a change of heart, Dana would be powerless to implement them in a consistent way and would continue to be ruled by her feelings of anxiety, anger, or guilt. First, Dana needed to understand herself better and what drove her heart to fear conflict and crave approval from others.

What Does Our Heart Worship?

God has created human beings as worshipers, and everyone worships something or someone. Once while speaking on this topic, a woman briskly informed me that she wasn't into worship, meaning she didn't like to go to church or sing hymns.

Worship is much deeper than a Sunday morning nod toward God or singing a few hymns in church. What we truly worship orients our everyday lives. We see it as our source of truth, hope, and well-being. God knows that what our heart loves the most will be the object of our worship. That's why he tells us to love him with all of our heart, all of our mind, all of our soul, and all of our strength (Mark 12:28-30). God wants to be our first love and he is the only one worthy of our worship (Revelation 2:4; Luke 4:8). God knows that many times people pretend to worship and love him, when in reality, they love something (or someone) else more. Jesus lamented about the pretense of the Pharisees when he said, "These people honor me with their lips, but their hearts are far from me" (Matthew 15:8). Their worship was in vain.

Dana was a Christian. She said she loved God. She went to church weekly and taught a women's Bible study. Dana did love God, but God was not her first love. Dana had other loves that took God's place in her heart. She worshiped and bowed down to the love and approval of people. Dana was people centered, not God centered. These other loves have a name: God calls them idols (Isaiah 44:17).

The apostle Paul warns us of this when he says that by nature we tend to exchange the truth of God for a lie, worshiping and serving created things (people or objects) more than God (Romans 1:25). Dana lived for people's love and approval and it ruled her life. She dreaded people's rejection or displeasure far more than she feared God's displeasure. When people loved her and were happy with her, she felt great. When they didn't, she became a wreck. As long as Dana

believed she *needed* their love and approval to live her life in a meaningful way, she would stay shackled to her fears. Proverbs tells us that
fearing others is a snare that will trap us (Proverbs 29:25).

A Change of Heart

For Dana to grow into the woman God created her to be and learn
to handle her interpersonal conflicts, she first needed to address the
sin exposed in her own heart and repent. Today we don't often like
to hear the words "sin" and "repent." They make us feel uncomfortable, but Jesus speaks so often in the Gospels about sin and repentance that it is important that we know what they mean. God says
we sin whenever we turn from what he tells us is true, good, and right
and instead substitute what we think is best, right, and good, or do
what we want to do instead of what he tells us. Eve did this in the
garden when she chose to eat the fruit, believing the serpent's lie over
what God said. In that moment she thought she knew better than
God about what would make her life work best and, therefore, disobeyed what God told her.

The Bible tells us that everyone sins because we all have disobeyed
God and gone our own way (Isaiah 53:6). Biblical repentance involves
more than feeling sorry or regretful about those choices or behaviors. It involves turning away from our sin *and* turning toward God.
We confess that our ways aren't true and don't work and that God's
ways are always true, good, and right. Repentance occurs in our heart
and involves our entire being, emotions, mind, and will.

In order for Dana to become a God-centered woman and learn
how to deal with interpersonal difficulties in a wise and godly way,
she will need to turn away from her idolatry of worshiping people
and their approval of her. She will need to turn her heart away from
fearing their disapproval and rejection so that she can become free
to turn toward God and to love him and be all he calls her to be.

To start this process, Dana agreed with God that she was captured by the fear of man, and she asked him to set her free. Dana
confessed that she loved the praise of people more than God, and
she now wanted to change this long-standing way of life. She invited

God to be her first love and desired to know and please him with all her heart.

Shortly after Dana made this commitment to God, her mother asked Dana to bring the children down to her home for the weekend. Gathering all her courage, Dana told her mother no, because she was tired and they all needed some family time. Her mother's cold silence and deep sigh of disapproval immediately triggered Dana's familiar feelings of anxious dread and guilt. Tempted to back down, she almost gave in to her mother's request in order to keep peace, but she quickly reminded herself (her thoughts) that she no longer wanted her life controlled by someone else's approval or disapproval. Dana chose (her will) to stand firm in her decision, regardless of what her mother thought or did in response.

Dana also chose to respond to her mother's cold disapproving sigh with kindness by saying, "Mom, I know you're disappointed, but I think this is best for the children and for our family this weekend. Another time will work better for us. Please understand."

As Dana made these changes, she felt uncomfortable because she wasn't used to putting God first instead of her mother or her husband's feelings or desires. Dana's new decision to put God in the center of her life did not mean that her husband or her mother's feelings or needs were no longer important to her. Loving God first never excludes loving others. Rather, it frees us to love them well instead of worrying about whether they love us back or not. God gives us his wisdom to see what is best, and we are empowered to do it without fear that someone will be angry or disappointed in us.

Causes of Conflict

There are many reasons why conflict occurs between people. We have personality differences, have different values or ideas, see things differently, and want different things in life. For example, I like to go to the beach and relax on vacation. I'd be happy reading novels and lounging the entire week. My husband hates that. He likes to keep busy, touring and visiting the sites. Neither is wrong, but over the years we have had to negotiate and discuss our different ideas of what constitutes a great vacation and compromise with each other.

When conflict gets ugly, it always involves some sort of sin. Many couples come for counseling because of intense marital conflict. They say, "We have a communication problem," but the real problem isn't communication. They know how to speak to each other just fine, even kindly when they want something. The problem is that when they fight, each of them wants their own way (the sins of selfishness and/or pride) and neither of them listens or gives respectful consideration to the other person's feelings or point of view. They argue because each is only looking out for his or her own interests, not the interests of their partner.

In the Bible James asks, "What causes fights and quarrels among you?" He answers that conflict arises because we don't get what we want and so we go to war and fight with one another to get it (James 4:1-2). The apostle Paul worried that he would find people in the church fighting with one another and said, "I fear that there may be quarreling, jealousy, outbursts of anger, factions, slander, gossip, arrogance and disorder" (2 Corinthians 12:20). Paul reminds us that "the entire law is summed up in a single command: 'Love your neighbor as yourself'" (Galatians 5:14). He warns, "If you keep on biting and devouring each other, watch out or you will be destroyed by each other" (verse 15). We are wise to avoid such sinful interactions. Constant bickering and quarreling will ruin any relationship and should not be the way Christians communicate with one another, even when they disagree.

Dana's primary strategy of shutting down and sticking her head in the sand, especially when there were important issues at stake, wasn't the biblical answer either. When she couldn't stand suppressing her feelings anymore, Dana blew up, but her angry outbursts only made things worse. People were hurt, everyone retreated and felt misunderstood, and the problems never were discussed or resolved.

Women often tell me, "I'm afraid to speak up and tell someone how I really feel about something because I'm scared if I do, he or she won't like me and then I'll be all alone." But as we have already seen, a relationship on those terms hardly qualifies as a healthy relationship. Other women tell themselves that someone else's anger or disapproval (even if temporary) is unbearable. Rather than fighting for an improved relationship by speaking the truth in love, they stay "nice" and passive, gradually becoming more and more disconnected from their own feelings and desires until they no longer know what they are. When a woman habitually relates with others in this way, she allows her spirit to deaden and eventually she may find herself depressed.

Sometimes a woman becomes very angry after pretending for so long that everything is fine. Once she allows this anger to grow, she no longer cares if anyone gets mad at her. Exploding, she lashes out in a desperate effort to communicate. "I'm sick of this and I want something to be different!" Sadly, the people in her life often trivialize her explosive anger. Minimizing it, they say to themselves, "She's having a bad day" or "She's under stress; she doesn't really mean what she said" or "It's that time of the month, so ignore her." Confusing things further, later on she often regrets the way she blurted out her ugly feelings and feels ashamed and guilty, so she backs down and tries even harder to accommodate and to make things work.

I don't advocate angry outbursts as a good strategy for initiating change in painful relationships or for resolving conflict. However, our angry feelings often signal that we're not happy with the way things are and that real change may be necessary for a relationship to continue. You are not alone in your struggle to handle relationship problems and conflicts in a godly way. Here are a few other women who feel just like you:

> *Anyone who shows disapproval in me causes me to spiral down, and my pattern has been to "write such ones off" instead of working through the process of reconciliation and agreement. Now I am trying to work things through …sometimes it's hard work!*   *~ Alice*

I've learned that being a Christian wife doesn't mean being a doormat and letting people walk all over you. I've learned I can be submissive and still be assertive in a loving way. I've learned that there is a fair way to fight and a right and wrong way to communicate. WOW. I've learned that it's okay to not always like the differences you have with your spouse, but I learned that my way isn't the right way, either. I learned that a marriage is give-and-take, and if you only give 50-50 and not 100 percent, it won't work. I learned that the tongue is a powerful weapon that can wreak havoc on a marriage if you're not careful. I learned that words can hurt more than physical harm.   *~Joy*

One of the things I think contributed to my depression is being manipulated by my spouse and not having the guts to stand up for myself. I've learned that I can survive conflict and that I need to deal with issues instead of letting them eat me up inside.   *~Lois*

Skills for Resolving Conflict

Now that we've looked at why we get so caught up in people pleasing and what needs to change in us first, we can identify the basic skills necessary to discuss difficult issues and differences in a God-honoring way.

Be Direct: Say How You Feel and Ask for What You Want

Many misunderstandings and conflicts arise because we never tell someone how we truly feel or ask for what we want. We assume the other person knows or should know those things without us having to say them. But trust me, they don't. Women are taught to communicate indirectly and, most of the time, people in our lives, especially men, don't get it. For example, when taking a long trip I used to say to my husband, "Are you hungry yet?" What I really meant by that question is "I'm hungry. Let's find a place to eat." But that felt too bold, too direct, too selfish, so instead I asked him if he was hungry. Unfortunately, he often answered, "Nope, not yet." And then I sat and starved, waiting until he decided he was hungry enough to stop.

When I wanted to enlist his help on the weekend, I said, "What are you doing this weekend?" He always had plenty he wanted to do, so then I wouldn't ask him to help me. Now I've learned to say, "There is a lot of yard work that needs to be done; I'd like you to be available to help on Saturday." There are times when he says, "That's fine" and other times when he says, "I can't. I planned something else." But at least I've asked and he's responded. That's a good starting place to begin negotiation and/or compromise.

Another problem I see when I encourage women to be more direct in asking for what they want is that they feel it's selfish to ask. Asking directly for what we want or need is not being selfish; it's being honest. When Dana's mother asked Dana to bring the children down to her home for the weekend, she was not being selfish, she honestly expressed her desire to see her grandchildren. It's when she didn't allow Dana's needs and feelings to count that she became selfish.

The Bible tells us that we are to "look not only to our own interests, but also to the interests of others" (Philippians 2:4). It never says we are *not* to look out for our own interests. Asking for what you want or desire, or expressing how you feel, is not selfish. Demanding that everyone *always give you what you want* is selfish. No one always gets everything he or she wants, but it is not selfish to have legitimate desires or want something God says is good for us to want.[1] We are, however, also to be considerate and thoughtful in regard to what someone else wants. That allows loving communication and compromise to occur.

If you never ask for what you want or never share how you feel, but find yourself resenting not getting what you want or growing tired of being in a lopsided relationship, then you must start to take responsibility for your own passivity. When we start to make a change and speak up, a conflict may occur because what we want is not what someone else wants. That brings us to our next skill—careful listening.

Listen Carefully and Respectfully to What Someone Else Wants

There are always at least two sides to every issue, two different perspectives on how to see something. If we want to have loving relationships, we must accept that our perspective might not always be the only way to see things, and it might not even be the best way. God has put us into relationships not only to meet our human desires for intimacy and companionship, but also so that we may grow, mature, and learn how to love better. One of the ways we love is to listen carefully and respectfully to someone else's feelings, thoughts, needs, dreams, and desires.

James tells us that we are to be quick to listen, slow to speak, and slow to become angry (James 1:19). One way to show that we're listening is through our body language. Face the person and look in his or her eyes. Turn off the television or other distractions. By doing so you are communicating, "What you're feeling or thinking is important to me, and I want to try to see things from your perspective."

After carefully listening, it is a good idea to paraphrase what you think you heard the other person saying. This helps to facilitate communication in two ways. First, if you've misunderstood what was said, it readily becomes apparent and can be corrected. Second, when you've correctly understood the other person's feelings or what she wanted and communicated them back to her, she feels heard and understood, even if you disagree or can't accommodate what she wants.

For example, when Dana heard her mother sigh after Dana told her that the children couldn't come for the weekend, Dana's response showed that she heard her mother's disappointment and cared about how she felt. She didn't give in to her mother's manipulation, but she did show compassion for her feelings.

Aim for a Win-Win Solution

Some conflicts are solvable and temporary and others may be more chronic, but when possible, look for a solution that both parties can live with and feel good about. For those who are married, sometimes we misunderstand biblical headship and submission to mean that the husband always gets his way in every conflict or disagreement. God never describes headship in that way. In fact, Jesus sternly cautions those in authority over others not to misuse their positions for selfish purposes (Mark 10:42-43). Godly headship always leads to sacrificial servanthood, not demanding one's own way.

To work together toward a mutually agreeable solution, whether it is a marital conflict or a disagreement among family members or friends, you must define the problem you're working to solve. For example, Dana felt angry because Ted spent money without telling her, but why was that a problem? Was it because she didn't think that was fair, or was it because she didn't like what he bought? Dana needed to think about why Ted's spending was a problem for her. As she looked at the situation more closely, she saw that the problem was what happened to her budget when Ted overspent. As Dana defined her problem and communicated directly how she felt and what she wanted, she may have said, "Ted, I don't like it when you spend money without telling me first. It throws our budget off and then I'm scrambling to find money to pay the bills. I'd like you to talk with me before you make a purchase over fifty dollars."

Dana defined the problem and asked Ted directly for the changes she wanted him to make. She told him how she felt without assaulting his character with ugly words like, "You're so irresponsible. How could you be so selfish?" As she listened to his response, Dana needed to show respect and consideration for Ted's feelings and a willingness to work with him to find a mutually acceptable solution to her problem of not having sufficient money to pay bills with. Sometimes this feels like very hard work. It is, and this work is what builds better and closer relationships.

This is the kind of work that allows my husband and me to go on vacation even when our preferences are very different. We talk about how we will spend our time together, being considerate of each other's desires, so that at the end of the vacation we've both had a good time.

Commit to Do No Harm

We have already learned that our words are powerful and they can be used to help and heal or to hurt and attack another person. Commit to God that you will not use your tongue as a weapon to harm someone else (Matthew 5:22). If you are unable to restrain your words because you are too angry or hurt, take some time out until you can. Make a plan to return to the issue when you are in a better frame of mind or can emotionally handle the discussion. Do return to it. Don't ignore it, hoping it will go away (Ephesians 4:25-26; Matthew 5:23-24). My pastor once said, "You can sweep broken glass under the rug but it will always work its way back up and eventually cut your foot."

If married couples, families, and friends would practice these basic interpersonal skills, ugly conflict would significantly decrease from their relationships.

When There Seems to Be No Solution to a Conflict

There are times when you do all you can, but there seems to be no resolution to the conflict. This often puts a strain on the relationship, but it doesn't have to. For example, Dana and her mother may permanently disagree on what's best for Dana's children, but as long as Dana is able to say no and her mother respects Dana's no, even if she disagrees with it, they can still have a good relationship. It's when Dana can't say no and inwardly resents her mother, or her mother refuses to accept Dana's no that their disagreements will ruin their relationship. There are many times we can agree to disagree and leave the conflict alone yet still get along with one another. However, there are times when the other person won't listen, talk, compromise, or even agree that there is a problem and you feel stuck. What should we do then?

The first thing we can always do is pray. Prayer doesn't always change a situation, but it can change the way we look at it. Let it go and trust God to work in the other person's heart (Matthew 5:44).

Second, work on being willing to forgive the other person if they have offended you or hurt you in any way. Let go of unresolved anger or bitterness so you don't allow Satan to get a foothold in your heart (Ephesians 4:27). The devil may have influenced the other person. Don't allow him to influence you too (Romans 12:19-21).

Third, achieving peace is not up to you alone. The Bible tells us that as much as it depends on us, we should be at peace (Romans 12:18), and we are to work toward preserving unity (Ephesians 4:3), but sometimes the other person is unwilling. In those instances, we must recognize and accept our limitations.

Last, we are to overcome evil with good (Romans 12:21). That does not mean that we can overpower another person's will or choices, but it does mean that we must guard our own heart so that the evil that has been done to us does not change us into someone who responds with more evil. When this happens Satan wins and both individuals in the conflict lose. When we surrender not only the outcome of conflict to God but also accept that God sometimes uses difficult things (including people) to mature us, then we can look for the good and respond with godly love, even when someone sins against us or we are in a difficult relationship.

Keep in mind that when someone refuses to accept responsibility for the ways they damage the relationship or the ways they hurt us, we can love them, but a close, mutually caring relationship with them is impossible.

Learning to Be Direct

Something to Think About

One of the biblical stories that always intrigued me is the story Jesus told his disciples of the ten virgins and their oil lamps (Matthew 25:1-13). They all went out to meet the bridegroom, but five of them were foolish and didn't take adequate oil to replenish their lamps. When the bridegroom took a long time coming, they all fell asleep. When midnight came and the bridegroom arrived, they trimmed their lamps and the five foolish women didn't have enough oil for the journey. They said to the five other women, who were better prepared, "Give us some of your oil; our lamps are going out." Stop reading for a moment and think about what you would do if you were facing the same dilemma.

A nice girl would give up some of her oil, even if that meant she ran short herself, even when she knew that the other women were irresponsible in not bringing adequate supplies for their journey. She would make this choice because she wouldn't want anyone to be angry with her, and she would want everyone to like her. She would not want to cause conflict and be rejected from the group. But in this story, that's not what these five women did.

Jesus says that the five wise women said no to the other women. They explained their reason and gave them a solution to their problem. They said, "There may not be enough for both us and you. Instead, go to those who sell oil and buy some yourselves." Jesus did not rebuke the wise women for saying no, nor did he call them selfish or stingy when they refused to give up their oil. They understood that their resources were limited and allocated them appropriately.

It wasn't up to the wise women to fix the problem when the other women had acted foolishly. It is important to learn that it is not always wrong or selfish to say no to someone. In fact, it may be what Jesus would want us to do.

Something to Do

One of the most useful skills I teach my clients who are learning how to express their feelings or confront problems is the "I statement." Here are two different ways Dana could have described her feelings and her concerns to Ted about his spending problem:

1. "Ted, I have a problem. I get upset when you spend money without checking with me first. Sometimes I don't have enough money to pay our bills. I'd like for you to check with me before you purchase something over fifty dollars. Can you do that for me?"

2. "Ted, you're driving me crazy when you spend money without telling me. You don't even think of how that will impact our budget. How can you be so irresponsible and thoughtless?"

Which approach do you think made a discussion with Ted more probable? In the first example, Dana didn't demean Ted or accuse him of wrongdoing. She stated clearly what she was feeling and asked for a specific change. In the second example, Ted likely responded by becoming defensive and arguing with Dana or throwing back some of his own criticisms.

Here are some "I statements" you can practice using:

I want or I'd like (describe as specifically as you can).

I want to go to the mountains for vacation this year.

I'd like to see a chick flick tonight.

I'd like you to help me cook dinner tonight. I'm tired.

I don't want, or I don't like (describe as specifically as you can what you don't like or want to be different).

I don't want company tonight.

I don't like it when you swear at me. It makes me feel disrespected and unloved.

I feel (emotion) when (describe an unacceptable behavior or attitude) and I'd like you to (describe a specific change you'd like to see).

I feel hurt when you are constantly interrupting me when I talk with you. I'd like you to give me five minutes of uninterrupted time to listen to me while I'm talking.

I feel angry when you leave all your dirty clothes all over the floor, and I'd like you to clean them up before we go to bed.

Mom, I have a problem. I feel guilty and anxious when you tell me I'm too strict or too protective with my children. I'd like it so much if you could try to support my parenting decisions. It would mean a lot to me.

Be sure when you're describing a problem that you describe a behavior or a specific attitude versus an overall character quality. For example here's an "I statement" that digresses into a global criticism. You're not likely to get much cooperation when you say something like this:

I feel angry when you leave all your dirty clothes all over the floor. You're such a slob.

Or

Mom! I'm so hurt. Can't you ever say anything nice? It's never good enough for you, is it?

Remember, pick a good time to talk about the issue when possible. Be specific with what your problem is and the changes you'd like to see. Avoid using words such as "always" or "never." Be considerate of the other person's feelings and point of view and work toward reconciling the relationship, even if the problem remains unresolved.

Very few conflicts are worth ending a relationship over. Don't turn minor issues into major battles. No one always gets everything he or she wants. When all else fails and there is a significant impasse, enlist the help of other believers, such as a Christian counselor, your pastor, or other wise people in the church. The apostle Paul pleaded with Euodia and Syntyche to settle their disagreement and asked others in the body of Christ to help them (Philippians 4:2-3).

Relationship difficulties can contribute to the overall stress in life. Growing through depression means acquiring the skills necessary to create and maintain godly relationships and facilitate connections with others. But as we have already learned, no human relationship can ever give us everything we need or make us totally happy. Let's now turn our attention to the things that hinder a dynamic relationship with God and learn how he may use our battle with depression for our good and his glory.

Part Three

A Woman's
Relationship
with God

Connecting with God

My guilt has overwhelmed me
Like a burden too heavy to bear.
PSALM 38:4

Save me, O God, for the waters have come up to my neck,
I sink in the miry depths, where there is no foothold.
I have come into the deep waters; the floods engulf me.
I am worn out calling for help; my throat is parched,
my eyes fail, looking for my God.
PSALM 69:1-3

I sought the LORD, *and he answered me;*
he delivered me from all my fears.
PSALM 34:4

Throughout this book my prayer has been that you have drawn closer to the heart of God, and that you have found him lovingly faithful, even while depressed. Sadly, depressed women withdraw from God, just as they withdraw from people. Sometimes they feel too weary, too numb, too hopeless, or too angry to talk to God. Others don't draw near to him because they feel guilty and ashamed, and fear God is disappointed with them. They believe (or have been told) that depression is unacceptable for a Christian and therefore their depression is a sin.

Is Depression a Sin?

People who are depressed are sinners, just as people are who aren't depressed. The Bible tells us, "For all have sinned; all fall short of God's glorious standard" (Romans 3:23 NLT). Getting depressed is not a sin any more than getting heart disease, AIDS, or cancer is, although sin (our own or the sin of others) may be a contributing factor. As we have already seen, depression is a condition that is triggered by a number of variables, such as physical vulnerabilities, stress, personal beliefs about self and life, environmental hardships, relationship difficulties, and yes, sinful lifestyle patterns (see diagram below). On the other hand, there are many individuals who recklessly sin or don't take care of themselves and don't get depressed, heart disease, AIDS, or cancer. We must not be simplistic and always assume that there is a causative relationship between sin and depression.

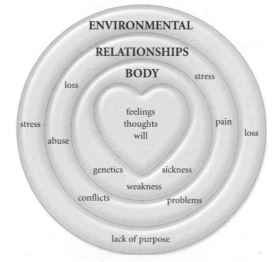

But I would be remiss if I didn't mention that for some individuals, even those who aren't professing Christians, depression can be triggered when they act in ways that ignore or oppose their core values or conscience. Let me give you an example.

A number of years ago, a distraught woman stopped by a local Christian bookstore asking for the name of a counselor. They handed her my card, and she called my office insisting on my first available appointment. When I saw her, Suzie looked thin and haggard. She had trouble sleeping and eating, and she also felt guilty, anxious, and afraid. When I inquired more about Suzie's background, she told me that she was the head nurse on the OB-GYN ward of a nearby hospital, and over the past few weeks, she had been having terrible nightmares. In her dreams baby ghosts would be chasing her, crying and asking her to help them. Suzie was terrified to go to sleep at night. She dreaded more nightmares.

Suzie's responsibilities at work involved assisting doctors who performed abortions, including mid-trimester abortions (those performed after 12 weeks gestation). Suzie wasn't a Christian, and she supported a woman's right to choose. She had offered to help with the abortion patients when other nurses had refused. Over time, Suzie discarded hundreds of lifeless babies, the grim consequences of a woman's right to choose. This dimension of her job bothered her, but she continued overruling her conscience, telling herself she was doing a good thing by helping women receive safe abortions. Until the nightmares started.

Suzie's internal warning bells were flashing full tilt, and if she continued to ignore them with her rationalizations, she was going to get physically, emotionally, and spiritually sicker. Sin always brings separation from God, which also leads to separation from others and ourselves. God is radically committed to loving us. That is why he tells us the truth about sin and what hinders our relationship with him. Telling us these things is not meant to make us merely feel guilty or to hurt our feelings but to show us what is true so that God becomes the center of our universe instead of ourselves. When we respond to God's truth and love in sincere repentance, we turn from our sin and toward him.

God used this frightening experience to bring Suzie into a personal relationship with himself. The psalmist says, "When we were overwhelmed by sins, you forgave our transgressions" (Psalm 65:3). Suzie's sleeplessness, guilt, and dread soon dissipated when she acknowledged her sin, received God's forgiveness, and requested to be reassigned to a new position at the hospital. Had she not listened, I have no doubt Suzie would have suffered a serious episode of depression.

In the Old Testament, King David was a man who was depression prone. He wrote many of the psalms I have included in this book. One of his most painful episodes of depression was triggered after he used his powerful position as king to pressure a married woman into having sexual relations with him. Later, when she told him she was pregnant, King David arranged for her husband to be killed in battle to cover up his sin. He knew what he was doing was wrong, yet he ignored God and his conscience and kept doing it. After a terrible bout of severe depression, this is what he wrote:

> Oh, what joy for those whose rebellion is forgiven, whose sin is put out of sight! Yes, what joy for those whose record the LORD has cleared of sin, whose lives are lived in complete honesty! When I refused to confess my sin, I was weak and miserable, and I groaned all day long. Day and night your hand of discipline was heavy on me. My strength evaporated like water in the summer heat. Finally, I confessed all my sins to you and stopped trying to hide them. I said to myself, "I will confess my rebellion to the LORD." And you forgave me! All my guilt is gone (Psalm 32:1-5 NLT).

David's life was frequented with recurrent bouts of depression, but only one of them appeared to be linked to his sin. But the Bible also describes David as a man after God's own heart (Acts 13:22). God loves us, even though we sin. King David's depression taught him to talk honestly with God about his situations, his feelings, and, when necessary, his sins. He eagerly went to God for comfort and help, for understanding and forgiveness, for love and compassion, and for wisdom. Don't let your depression or guilt over your sin keep you from God. He sees it, he understands it, and he wants to help you move beyond it.

> *Before I became depressed, I could talk about the love of God, his grace and mercy, and I could encourage anyone to follow him. Throughout my depression, I've experienced God's grace and mercy, whereas before, I could only talk about it. I have a lot more to learn.*
> *~Alice*

Hindrances in Connecting with God

Without a doubt the most important relationship we will ever have is our relationship with God. Only God can enter our deepest heart and heal our wounded and sin-sick soul. Only God can give us the unfailing love we so desperately crave. Only God can be our sure foundation, our rock, and our refuge in an upside-down, topsy-turvy world that, at times, makes no sense to our human understanding.

Many people, including depressed women, don't experience the reality of God. They don't see him as a very present help in times of trouble, or as their faithful Friend, Father, Shepherd, or King. Rather, they see him as distant and find it difficult to trust him or totally rely on him, even when things are going well in their lives.

Because intimate communion with God is so vital to our well-being now and eternally, let's look at some of the things that hinder deeper intimacy with God. These hindrances are true for all people, but for those caught in the darkness of depression, they make a relationship with God that much harder.

When depressed, it's extremely difficult to think clearly, and during those times it feels impossible to find, let alone draw comfort from, the reality and truth of who God is and what he tells us. I personally know what it feels like to not believe God's words and to believe other words that seem to speak much louder to me. I also know what it's like to be so mad at someone that I don't care what his or her words say, including God's. These are very real human struggles in our journey of faith. And I can assure you that I have come to know what it feels like to believe God's Word and cling to it in hope and trust—and that makes all the difference in how you experience life.

> *During my depression, I mostly saw God in the same way that I saw others—distant and displeased. I am beginning to see God as the Light and Savior that can lead me out of the depression and as the God of compassion, comfort, and faithful love.*   ~ Gwen

Unbelief

Everyone struggles with unbelief, even believers. We want to trust God but sometimes our own internal voices speak much louder so that we can't hear him or don't trust what he tells us is true.

Let's put unbelief in human terms. What kind of relationship would you have with someone if you didn't trust what he or she told you or didn't believe that they truly cared about you? When we distrust God and his concern for us, we can't feel close with him. It's impossible. The remedy for unbelief is trust. He tells us, "Trust me with your whole heart. Don't depend upon your own way of looking at things. In every way look for me and I will direct your steps" (Proverbs 3:5-6, my own paraphrase).

Jesus told his disciples, "Do not let your hearts be troubled. Trust in God; trust also in me" (John 14:1). Trust Jesus. This sounds too simple, yet Jesus tells us that when we trust him, we don't get so rattled by life (John 16:33). The opposite of trust is unbelief.

A.W. Tozer wrote, "Unbelief is a deadly sin. Among all created beings, not one dare trust in itself. God alone trusts in Himself, all other beings must trust in Him. Unbelief is actually perverted faith, for it puts its trust not in the living God but in dying man."[1]

Doubt is not the same as unbelief. God may use our doubt to build and refine our faith. However, when we struggle with doubt, if we're not careful, we can quickly slip into unbelief. Satan is more than happy to create severe turmoil in our life in an attempt to get us to disbelieve God's goodness and love for us (see Job 1:1-12).

Satan isn't the only one that sows seeds of doubt and unbelief. Our world has a way of thinking about life that is contrary to God's wisdom. When we feed ourselves a steady diet of worldly wisdom through what we read and watch on television, confusion and doubt creep in, often rendering us incapable of discerning what is true, good, right, and helpful (James 3:13-16).

We can do some things that make faith more likely to take root in the garden of our heart. One of those things is meditatively reading God's Word, just as we've been practicing throughout this book. When you come upon something in the Bible you struggle with, be honest with yourself. Ask God, "Do I trust what you're telling me here?" Ask him to show you your doubts and unbelief. What things are you afraid to believe him about? Where do you find yourself trusting in your own version of truth instead of what God tells you? Like the desperate young father in the biblical account, who wanted to believe God more, ask God to increase your faith (Mark 9:24). Then we must take that next step and choose to trust. Trust is an act of our will and in my life is often done minute by minute, decision by decision, incident by incident. Sometimes I find it easier than other times, but the more I journey along this faith walk, the more I trust God. He is faithful.

Another way I find that my faith grows is to spend more time in nature. Observing God's creation, his power, and his ordered orchestration of the universe reminds me of my smallness and his greatness and moves my heart to praise and worship. When I see all he has made and how wonderfully it all fits together, my faith increases and my willingness to trust God with the details of my life grows.

God loves it when we diligently seek him and choose to trust him. It delights his heart when his creation desires to know him and we yield ourselves in humble, childlike trust.

> *At times I've wondered where in the world he is...I'm now working on drawing closer to God emotionally.*
> *~ Wendy*

> *More times than not, when I was depressed I just held on unable to even pray. There were times of great doubt. You know, the big "WHY?" question. I know that depression changed my relationship with him...there was the doubt and I experienced anger. Why did this happen to me and why didn't he just take it all away? He could have! I slid backward in my spiritual life. Right now I think I am healing, not only from all that happened to me, but I'm healing in my relationship with the Lord. Of all the broken relationships in my life, this one hurt the most. I missed the closeness I once had with him. Now that I am able to look at myself and at all of the things that have happened, I know that he has shown me the truth about myself in each of these situations. It always was about me; I just didn't see it. I needed to know the truth so that I could be set free.*   *~ Karen*

Idolatry

In the Old Testament, the children of Israel didn't struggle only with unbelief but also with idolatry. Their hearts were drawn away from loving the true God, and they began worshiping other things, like a golden calf or a wooden pole. When we read these stories, we say to ourselves, "How stupid could they have been?" Yet, today we do the same things. Our idol isn't a golden calf, but it is gold or money. It may not be a wooden pole, but it might be the ladder of success or popularity.

One way I look for my idolatry is to be mindful of the things I love. Loving things other than God is not wrong, but God says that we are to love him first and most. Often my other loves aren't bad things; they're good things that I love too much. Richard Baxter, a Puritan preacher and biblical counselor in the 1600s, wrote, "Were nothing overloved, it would have no power to torment us."[2] One way we know whether we love something too much is to see how much power we give it to wreak havoc on our mental and emotional life when we think we might not get it.

As we have already seen, some women love approval and acceptance from others. Who doesn't love it when everyone thinks we're wonderful, but are we distraught when we don't receive approval? Do we become anxious and teary at the slightest hint of disapproval or rejection? Most of us love control and desire to have control over our lives and the people and things around us. But what happens to you and in you when you don't have control? Do you become angry, fearful, or despondent? These emotions can be good warning lights to remind us that we have allowed our heart to be captured by other loves, and we're trusting in our idol instead of in God. God says he is a jealous God and will show us our other loves (see Jeremiah 3), but he hates being second or third in our lives (Psalm 78:58). When we continue to love other things more than we love him, we forfeit our intimacy with him (Jonah 2:8). God won't be relegated to the position of a cosmic errand boy we call upon when we think we need him or want something. He wants to be our lover, our best friend, our King and our Lord.[3]

Having idols won't make you depressed, but they will distract you and keep you from intimacy and a deeper relationship with God. Depression is then set in motion when our idols disappoint us, as they always will. We have lost our first love, and we are undone. This will either draw our heart back toward God or make us bitter toward him.

God knows that we can only hold on to him with all of our heart when we have let go of everything else.

> *I have learned to depend upon God and not others for my happiness. I take time every evening for my quiet time—to pray, meditate, write in my journal, and read.*
>
> *~ Maxine*

> *My depression has forced me to look at myself, my flaws, my character defects, and my idols, and I'm more aware than ever of my need for God. It's not just about not drinking, nor is it about doing the right thing. It's about living the right way as God wants me to. I know God wants to comfort my soul if I would only remove the blocks myself.*
>
> *~ Sarah*

> *My relationship with God changed when I met him at the bottom of the barrel, at the end of my rope, and he said, "Come, follow me." I'm learning what it means to talk with God and to listen. I have learned what it means to love God first and not just with words or in my brain, but in my heart. He is my lifeline.*
>
> *~ Diane*

Bitterness

There is a huge difference between not understanding God, even complaining to him about our plight, and being bitter with him about it. Job experienced severe loss, great physical pain, and relationship difficulties that would trigger deep depression in most of us. Job was confused, hurt, and angry, but in all of this, Job did not become bitter toward God. Job spoke honestly about his feelings, all the while hoping in God's character (Job 13:15; 16:19-21; 19:25-27).

Although we'd be ashamed to admit it, some of us are in a relationship with God only for what he gives us. Our bitterness exposes this truth. So does our chronic grumbling and complaining. When

God doesn't come through for us as we'd like or expect him to, our bitterness says, "God, you've failed me. You do not love me very well. You're not giving me what I need to live my life the way I want or planned."

This was Jonah's response to God when God allowed the vine that sheltered him to wither. Jonah became so angry with God that he said, "I am angry enough to die" (Jonah 4:9). Through this loss, God was trying to show Jonah that their relationship was superficial and hindered by Jonah's self-centeredness and lack of love. Jonah desired God's favor and love for himself, but he didn't want to show God's compassion or love to others.

These painful experiences aren't meant to drive us from God, but to expose our sin and our incorrect or distorted view of him. Often, in our anger, we're not honestly looking for God. We're just looking for him to make things better for us or give us what we want. In order to remove this stumbling block, we must learn to humble ourselves, allowing God to be God and draw near to him so that he can change our heart.

Depression has a way of making everything look negative, even God's care for you. If you find yourself chronically angry and bitter with God, you can start to feel differently if you intentionally look for things you can be thankful for. He always loves you and cares for you, even when you're mad at him or involved with other loves, but you might not be noticing it or appreciating it in the midst of your depression. Each morning try to write in your journal at least three to five things you can thank God for. At the end of the day, review them and praise God for his love and care for you. Our relationship with others grows deeper and sweeter when we appreciate them and notice the little things they do for us. The same is true with God.

I've seen God care for me. He has not asked me to evangelize the world or any other grandiose thing. He has asked that I receive his care for me. I am most humbled

*at God ministering to me, when all along I've believed,
"Well, you did all that work on the cross. Now it's my
turn to minister and glorify you. You don't have to do
anything else for me." And, although God doesn't HAVE
to do anything else, he LONGS to, and that's the sweetest
thing I've learned about him.*   *~ Vickki*

*In the worst of my depression I didn't even see God, but
I clung to the hope of seeing him. In hindsight I feel he
was with me the whole time. Now my relationship with
him is filled with much gratitude and love on my part
for things that were given me without a doubt from no
one but God.*   *~ Edie*

*God seemed very distant during my depression. I prob-
ably didn't think too much about God because I was so
self-absorbed. There was some anger at him for allowing
the situations that caused the depression.*   *~Sue*

Disobedience

Jesus says clearly that we demonstrate our love for him by listening to him and obeying him (John 15:10), even when we doubt
his wisdom or don't understand why. We've all been in relationship
with someone who says one thing but does another. Talk is easy. When
that happens, we sometimes say, "Show me your love by your actions."
Jesus says the same thing to us. When we refuse to listen to what he
tells us, we not only suffer the consequences of our foolishness, we
forfeit intimacy with him as we move away from him to go our own
way (1 John 2:3-6).

Peter was an ordinary man, a local fisherman, impetuous and a
little rough around the edges. But Jesus saw great potential in Peter
and wanted a relationship with him. Early one morning Jesus was
standing by Lake Gennesaret teaching a crowd of people. Peter was
on shore, washing his nets after returning from a long unsuccessful

night of fishing. Bone tired, Peter was looking forward to heading home and crawling into bed, but Jesus had other plans. First he climbed right into Peter's boat and asked Peter to move it out a little from shore so he could teach the people. Surprised, Peter went along with the teacher's request. After Jesus was finished teaching, he told Peter to take his boat deeper and drop his nets for a catch.

As I put myself into this scene, I can imagine myself saying just what Peter said. "But Jesus, my nets are already all cleaned up. I'm exhausted. We were out there all night and didn't catch anything." Peter didn't *feel* like doing what Jesus asked him to do. He expressed his honest feelings to Jesus, but he went one step further. Peter added, "But because you say so, I will let down the nets" (see Luke 5:1-5 for the story).

Because you say so, I will do it. What a wonderful, endearing thing to say to Jesus. Can you imagine how delighted (or shocked) your mom would have been if just once you would have responded to her in this way? "Mom, because you say so, I will do it." Likewise, it thrills God when we respond to him in simple obedience.

> *Through depression I have acquired more self-knowledge, and I have grown in my knowledge of God and in my love for him. This has only come about since I stopped fighting against God and started accepting that his grace is sufficient for me and that his strength is made perfect in my weakness. My relationship with God has deepened and become more intimate.*   ~Cheryl

Misbelief

The final hindrance in experiencing our relationship with God is our ignorance of who God is and what his purposes are. As Rick Warren so wisely writes in his popular book *The Purpose-Driven Life*, "It's not about you. The purpose of your life is far greater than your own personal fulfillment, your peace of mind, or even your happiness."[4] Many people are disillusioned with their relationship with God because they have seen him as someone to help them reach their purposes for their life. When he doesn't cooperate the way they think he should, they lose faith, and sometimes lose hope.

When we deal with misbelief, one of the fundamental flaws in our relationship with God is that we don't know him as he is. We have created a caricature of God—a grossly distorted picture of who he is and what he does. The source of our information about God is our feelings, or our experiences, and we become the defining rod of truth, rather than believe what God says about who he is.

This misunderstanding of God and how he works threw me into deep depression after a severe loss in my life. After my son, Ryan, was born, we knew we'd be unable to have more children. I always hoped and prayed that God would give us a second child through adoption. Through a miraculous set of circumstances, I became acquainted with a woman, Sue, who had a friend looking for an adoptive family for her unborn child.

Sue introduced my husband and me to her pregnant friend, and we all agreed that we would adopt her baby when it was born, the due date being only two months away. The arrangements were made, the nursery decorated, and we eagerly waited for God's precious gift to us. But when the time came, Sue's friend didn't call us, and Sue was given the unpleasant task of telling us the bad news. This pregnant woman chose another couple to adopt her child without telling us. I was devastated. "How could God have allowed this to happen?" I cried. "He tricked me!" The pain I felt was beyond anything I had ever experienced. I felt horrified that this woman betrayed us. I grieved because I didn't receive the baby my heart longed for. But I can honestly say that the deepest and greatest torture to my soul came because I believed that God was not good. I told myself that he had deceived me. He stirred my longings and then dashed my hopes. I thought he enjoyed seeing me suffer.

I have since learned that God is not like I thought he was, but you would not have convinced me of that at the time. My view of him was distorted by my own feelings, wrong expectations, and past experiences. God knew that and was always lovingly at work, even when I didn't see him.

The Bible tells us who God is and explains him as best as he is going to be explained to our finite minds. Jesus showed us what God is like (Colossians 1:15). Much later, as I read God's Word and observed Jesus' interactions with people, I saw that he never took pleasure in people's pain or caused them meaningless suffering. I had to choose whose view of God I was going to rely on: My own or what Jesus showed me and God's Word told me. The psalmist says, "For with you is the fountain of life; in your light we see light" (Psalm 36:9).

Dr. J.I. Packer, a great teacher and theologian, wrote:

> Knowing about God is crucially important for the living of our lives…We are cruel to ourselves if we try to live in this world without knowing about the God whose world it is and who runs it. The world becomes a strange, mad, painful place, and life in it a disappointing and unpleasant business, for those who do not know about God. Disregard the study of God, and you sentence yourself to stumble and blunder through life, blindfolded, as it were, with no sense of direction and no understanding of what surrounds you. This way you can waste your life and lose your soul.[5]

When I first got depressed, I didn't even know God. Since then I've been saved and have a much better understanding of God and his Word.   ~ Kim

Part of my depression came from not knowing God's mercy and grace. I can say now, with the help of my Christian counselor, that I have full assurance that I am saved and forgiven through the blood of Jesus Christ. I can look back and see that God has been with me through

my depression, and he is growing me up in a new under-
standing of who he is.   *~Alice*

Before my depression...caused by a crisis in my mar-
riage...I perceived God as a distant Father, taking care
of my salvation, loving me, and showing up in various
blessings in my life. I would have glimpses of his "close-
ness." But in the real crisis time, he was close, loving. His
Spirit reached out to me, speaking words of tenderness
and comfort.   *~Gina*

Demonic Activity in Depression

Our relationship with God is extremely crucial in healing depression. However, I must warn you that there are other forces working
against you in addition to your own difficulties connecting with God.
We have a real enemy at work whose intention is to do all he can to
alienate us from God and destroy our lives. Satan does not want you
to get better.

We first see evidence of Satan at work in Genesis 3 where he twists
God's words and manipulates Eve so that she will begin to doubt
God's goodness and wisdom. Later we see him tormenting Job, insti-
gating a series of catastrophic losses and health problems just so that
Job will curse God and give up his faith (Job 1). Job was totally
unaware that a larger spiritual battle was being fought behind the
scenes of his suffering. In another biblical story, an angel of the Lord
was hindered from responding to Daniel's prayers because of Satan's
opposition (Daniel 10:12-13). Our enemy is fierce, the battle real.
The apostle Paul doesn't want us to be naive. He warns us:

> For our struggle is not against flesh and blood, but against
> the rulers, against the authorities, against the powers of
> this dark world and against the spiritual forces of evil in
> the heavenly realms (Ephesians 6:12).

One of the names of Satan is *diabolos,* which means "an accuser, a slanderer."[6] Depression's voice often slanders God's character, and at the same time it accuses us of all of our faults, sins, weaknesses, flaws, and shortcomings. Understand that Satan, who wants you destroyed or dead, is behind these internal accusations, fueling your insecurities so that they consume you (1 Peter 5:8-9).

I have seen demonic activity at work in every case where the client is entertaining suicidal thoughts. Women considering suicide have told me they struggle with thoughts like: "Go ahead, kill yourself. No one will miss you" or "You're just dragging everyone down around you. They'd all be better off if you were dead. Just make it look like an accident." Please understand that if this happens, you are being attacked and lied to. Jesus tells us Satan is a murderer, a liar, and a deceiver (John 8:44). *The truth is that your life is extremely precious to God and he loves you.*

If you are having any kind of suicidal thoughts, please tell someone and get help right now for your depression. Starting on page 238 you will find some phone numbers and a Christian online resource that will help you immediately with your suicidal thoughts and feelings. Your life is too valuable to throw away.

> *Without God and his Word, I don't know if I could have made it through. I went into a warfare mode, literally for my soul. I believe there were spiritual and physical things to deal with.*   ~ Veda

God's Word strongly urges us to, "Humble yourselves before God. Resist the Devil, and he will flee from you. Draw close to God and God will draw close to you" (James 4:7-8 NLT).

Choosing Surrender

Something to Think About

Did you ever wonder if Jesus felt depressed? He was described as a man of sorrows and acquainted with grief (Isaiah 53:3 NKJV). Some writers describe the Garden of Gethsemane as Christ's experience with depression. Jesus struggled with himself, he struggled with Satan, and he struggled with God. Never before in his entire ministry had Christ questioned the Father's will. He always eagerly conformed himself to whatever the Father wanted him to do or to say. This time was different. The Bible says Jesus "began to be filled with horror and deep distress." He told his disciples, "My soul is crushed with grief to the point of death" (Mark 14:33-34 NLT). He battled within himself, and he battled with the powers of darkness that tormented him, yet he did all this without sinning. His friends disappointed him and he felt alone. Jesus was in such "agony of spirit that his sweat fell to the ground like great drops of blood" (Luke 22:44 NLT). The horror of sin was so great that Jesus asked God whether he could find another way to accomplish his purposes.

Though Jesus struggled, he surrendered to God. He didn't just give in, the way one might surrender to an enemy that has just surrounded you with guns pointed. Jesus sincerely prayed, "Abba, Father, everything is possible for you. Please take this cup of suffering away from me. Yet I *want* your will, not mine" (Mark 14:36 NLT, emphasis added). Jesus willingly surrendered his apprehension and anguish to the sovereignty, goodness, and wisdom of Almighty God. After Christ's surrender, an angel strengthened him (Luke 22:43). Will you surrender your fear, sorrow, disappointment, unbelief, and bitterness?

Will you surrender anything and everything that keeps you from knowing and relying on the love God has for you?

Something to Do

If we look at Christ as our model, what can we learn about the experience of depression, and how to live in it and yet not sin?

First, accept that you will have sorrow. Life is hard, even when we love God. Jesus tells us that this world is full of troubles. Satan will use this time to cast doubt upon God's character. He might say, "How can God love you if he allows this to happen?" If our theology is weak or our relationship with God shallow, Satan can easily get the upper hand.

Many of the godliest people I know mourn deeply, not only for their own sins and sorrows, but also for the sins and sorrows of others. Their highly sensitized spirits experience the hurts of others as if they were their own hurts, and this affects their body and their mood. Understand that in these moments you are entering into the sufferings of Christ, and just as Jesus was, you are under spiritual attack when you feel tempted to doubt God. Guard your heart with the truth and put on the full armor of God (Ephesians 6:10-18).

Next, identify the struggle. The temptation to doubt or become angry with God initiates a struggle between our way and God's way and between good and evil. What is it that you want and are not getting? What are you fighting against? Our struggle is not sinful, but we must identify and unmask our enemy. Are we fighting to have our own way (pride), or are we battling against the lies and accusations of our enemy, Satan, who wants to destroy us?

Surrender to God. As quickly as you can, yield your heart (mind, emotions, and will) to him. Say, "Yes, Lord. I only want what you want." Jesus showed this was possible in his anguished garden prayer, and we are to do as he did. In my life I find this process needs to be repeated again and again because my surrender is often minute by minute.

Allow yourself to be strengthened. This is done through God's Word, the Holy Spirit, and fellow believers. As Elijah did, receive what truth and comfort God wants to give you to nourish you. Take a moment right now and read Isaiah 40:12-31. If you can, read it in a modern version such as *The Message* or the New Living Translation. Ponder who God is and what he is telling you about himself in this passage. Can you trust him and surrender to his wisdom? If you find yourself resisting, you're not finished struggling. Go back and identify the struggle.

Remember,

> That is why we have a great High Priest who has gone to heaven, Jesus the Son of God. Let us cling to him and never stop trusting him. This High Priest of ours understands our weaknesses, for he faced all of the same temptations we do, yet he did not sin. So let us come boldly to the throne of our gracious God. There we will receive his mercy, and we will find grace to help us when we need it (Hebrews 4:14-16 NLT).

Let Me Not Doubt

Let me not doubt
Thy coming and Thy going in my life;
Let me not doubt
Thy constant care and watching o'er me still
Thy dove of peace and comfort
o'ershadowing in the strife,
Thy torch of hope illumining
the darkness of Thy will.
But let me sing
the joyfulness of comfort in Thy Word;
The ringing of Thy faithful voice
familiar to my ears;

The light of love for me
resplendent in Thy face, O Lord;
The confidence of knowing
Thou are present everywhere.

L.M. MILES[7]

How Long, Lord, How Long?

How long, O LORD? Will you forget me forever?
How long will you hide your face from me?
How long must I wrestle with my thoughts
And every day have sorrow in my heart?
How long will my enemy triumph over me?
PSALM 13:1-2

Why, O LORD, do you stand far off?
Why do you hide yourself in times of trouble?
PSALM 10:1

I waited patiently for the LORD to help me,
and he turned to me and heard my cry.
He lifted me out of the pit of despair,
out of the mud and the mire.
He set my feet on solid ground and
steadied me as I walked along.
PSALM 40:1-2 NLT

One day a leper flung himself down before Jesus and pleaded to be healed. He begged, "Lord, if you are willing, you can make me clean" (Luke 5:12).

This desperate cry from the leper's heart was never a question of Christ's ability to heal him. Even in biblical times, good news traveled fast and Jesus' healing power was the talk of the town. This leper had no doubt whether Jesus was able to heal him, but he did fear that Jesus might not be willing to do so.

I am deeply moved by Jesus' response to this hopeless man. The first thing Jesus did was touch him. Christ's tender touch surprised him because lepers were never touched. The leper's boldness in approaching Jesus was also quite remarkable because lepers were shunned and ostracized from community life. Jesus reached down and touched the untouchable and reassured him with his words, "I am willing" (verse 13).

Jesus, Are You Willing to Heal Me?

You too may be desperate to be healed from depression or you probably wouldn't have picked up this book and read this far. Right now you may be feeling discouraged because Jesus hasn't healed you yet. But did you ever notice that Jesus didn't heal everyone in the same way? For some individuals, like the leper, he spoke a word and instantly they were healed. For others, he took more time.

For example, Jesus could have restored sight to a blind man with his words alone, but in one story he took the man outside the village, spit on his eyes, and then asked him what he saw. When the man told Jesus, "I see people, but I can't see them very clearly. They look like trees walking around," Jesus again placed his hands over the blind man's eyes. At last, his sight was completely restored (Mark 8:23-25 NLT).

When healing a second blind man, Jesus made a paste out of dirt and his saliva, packed it on the man's sightless eyes, and told him to go and wash in the Pool of Siloam. It was only after the man obeyed Jesus and went and washed that his sight was restored (John 9:6-7).

I wonder what would have happened to that second blind man if he had refused to go and wash. What if he had argued with Jesus about the way Jesus chose to heal him? He might have said, "Jesus, I don't understand you. Why don't you just say the word like you did with the leper? Why do you have to do it this way? I don't like mud in my eyes, especially mud mixed with human saliva. It stinks!

How can you expect me to find that pool all by myself and wash when I'm still blind? Why are you so cruel?"

Fortunately, the blind man was not so foolish as to argue with the wisdom of Jesus. But sometimes I have not been so wise or so obediently trusting. I have argued with God and said all of those imagined words (and more), especially when he hasn't healed me when I wanted him to or changed my situations the way that I thought he should. I haven't always done what he's told me to do to get better and, besides, I hate waiting.

You've probably longed to feel God's touch upon your heart or to hear his words, "I am willing," but all you hear lately is dead silence. Or perhaps you have heard from God, but you didn't like what he said to do or to change. You've resisted and argued with him or have not done the things that he has told you to do to get better. Your pride or your shame keeps you captured in the same old ruts of life. You've wanted God to make you better, but on your terms. Now you're afraid he's given up on you.

We all struggle with these fears. We believe in God's power, but we doubt his goodness, mercy, and grace. When we don't see him directly and immediately working on our behalf, we often feel unloved and rejected. We erroneously conclude that God is not willing, I must not be worth it to him, or he is angry and disgusted with me. *But that is not true.* Please hear this. When Jesus didn't heal someone immediately, or at all, it was *never, ever* because he didn't love the person or care about his or her suffering. (Remember the story of Lazarus and Mary and Martha in chapter 1?)

If God delays in healing your depression, first ask yourself whether you have listened to what he has been telling you to do to start getting well (perhaps through reading this book). If you've been resisting him or refusing to obey, what stands in the way? You can't do battle with something that you don't face up to and admit.

But if you've prayed and listened and obeyed as best you can but still feel the heaviness of depression engulfing you, you must learn to cling to the assurance that there are other purposes at work beyond what you can see right now.

When God Waits

Charles Haddon Spurgeon, a renowned preacher, prolific author, and beloved pastor during the 1800s, battled depression throughout his life. He was refreshingly honest with his struggle and never pretended he didn't feel what he felt. Yet he always found hope in looking for God's purposes in it.

Please don't misunderstand me here. Even when you correctly grasp the purposes of God, right answers never take away your suffering or even lessen it. However, an accurate knowledge and understanding of what God might be up to makes it easier for you to keep your eyes on him in the midst of your pain, which is a big help. Answers are important because they increase our hope that there is some purpose and meaning to our continued battle with depression, but correct answers will never comfort us when we're crushed with suffering. Comfort is experienced through a loving community of friends and family.

I want to help you understand some of the reasons God may not heal you right away or why he allows your depression to return. Because it's hard to think clearly while depressed, it is essential during times when you're not as depressed to continue training your mind to think correctly about God and his ways. I don't expect you to like some of the reasons God waits or to fully understand his purposes. God doesn't expect you to, either; he only asks you to trust him. Remember, faith is not about what we can see and touch but about what is unseen (Hebrews 11:1).

The Bible tells us that God is eternal and that he doesn't measure things in clock time the way we do. To him one day is like a thousand years and a thousand years is like a day (2 Peter 3:8). When we don't see God working in human clock time, he is working; only he works in mysterious ways and in his own time.

In the wonderful *When God Weeps*, the authors wrote,

> Our pain, poverty, and broken hearts are not his ultimate
> focus. He cares about them, but they are merely symp-
> toms of the real problem. God cares most—not about
> making us comfortable—but about teaching us to hate
> our sins, grow up spiritually, and love him. To do this,
> he *gives us salvation's benefits only gradually, sometimes
> painfully gradually.* In other words, he lets us continue
> to feel much of sin's sting while we're headed for heaven.[1]

Why? What could be God's purposes for allowing those he loves
to continue to suffer? Following are just a few of them.

God Uses Suffering to Tenderize Us

Let me ask you a question. Who knows best how to talk with a
depressed woman who has lost all hope? Is it a woman who has everything together and has all the answers or a depressed woman who
is trusting God in the midst of her depression? A woman who knows
the comfort of God while suffering depression is able to comfort and
speak to another woman in a way those who have never walked on
that path can.

The apostle Paul assures us that our suffering has a purpose and
is used by God, not only in our own lives, but also to help others.
He writes,

> All praise to the God and Father of our Master, Jesus the
> Messiah! Father of all mercy! God of all healing counsel!
> He comes alongside us when we go through hard times,
> and before you know it, he brings us alongside someone
> else who is going through hard times so that we can be
> there for that person just as God was there for us (2 Co-
> rinthians 1:3-4 MSG).

Charles Spurgeon knew this was one of the purposes of his frequent depressions. He wrote the following about it:

I often feel very grateful to God that I have undergone fearful depression of spirits. I know the borders of despair, and the horrible brink of that gulf of darkness into which my feet have almost gone; but hundreds of times I have been able to give a helpful grip to brethren and sisters who have come into that same condition, which grip I could never have given if I had not known their deep despondency.[2]

Oswald Chambers wrote of the value of our experiences,

If you are going to be used by God, He will take you through a multitude of experiences that are not meant for you at all, they are meant to make you useful in His hands, and to enable you to understand what transpires in other souls so that you will never be surprised at what you come across.[3]

Puritan theologian Thomas Kelly also knew of God's purposes in suffering. He reminds us: "The heart is stretched through suffering and enlarged. But O the agony of this enlarging of the heart, that one may be prepared to enter into the anguish of others."[4]

The shame of depression often makes us feel like a social leper. We don't think we have anything to offer, and we lurk in the borders and shadows of community life. If God permits you to suffer depression, please understand that he has a purpose behind it, and one of the reasons may be that he will use you in a special way to minister and care for others. In his book *The Purpose-Driven Life*, Rick Warren said,

If you really desire to be used by God, you *must* understand this powerful truth: The very experiences that you have resented or regretted most in life—the ones you've wanted to hide and forget—are the experiences God wants to use to help others. They *are* your ministry![5]

To use your experiences to help others you must stop hiding the fact that you are depressed. Instead, own it, work through it, and let God use it to help others. Spurgeon encourages us when he said, "There are none so tender as those who have been skinned themselves. Those who have been in the chamber of affliction know how to comfort those who are there."[6]

> *I am more compassionate with people and am able to see through behaviors to the heart.*   ~*Laura*

> *I have become a better person having gone through depression. I am closer to the Lord and have a better understanding of the reasons we humans are put on this earth. I am still in search of my specific purpose in life, but I do understand that God gives me experiences to prepare me for my purpose.*   ~*Donna*

God Uses Suffering to Strengthen Us

No one feels strong when they are suffering, yet the paradox and mystery of suffering is that when we allow it, the process itself strengthens us.

I like to work out with weights, or perhaps more honestly, I like the results of working out with weights. The workouts themselves are painful, and I feel weak when I struggle to lift my heavier weights. But if I only do my workout with light weights, I won't grow stronger. James tells us the same thing when he says that we can actually experience joy in the midst of hardship, because we know that our trials are developing internal spiritual muscles that will make us more beautiful to God and help us run the race of faith with endurance (James 1:2 5).

The apostle Paul discovered that embedded in his weakness was God's strength (2 Corinthians 12:9-10). Paul encourages all believers when he writes,

> We can rejoice, too, when we run into problems and trials,
> for we know that they are good for us—they help us learn
> to endure. And endurance develops strength of character
> in us, and character strengthens our confident expecta-
> tion of salvation (Romans 5:3-4 NLT).

No one would choose deep suffering as a pathway for spiritual or emotional growth. We'd rather learn with easier lessons. But God is always more concerned with our growth than our temporal happiness. Therefore, he sometimes thrusts us into the classroom of personal and experiential suffering. It's one thing to read about how to do something in a book, it's another to have to actually learn to do it. That's why it is so vital that we pay attention and learn what he's teaching us so that our suffering produces those mental, emotional, and spiritual muscles God intends for us to develop.

> *During my depression I not only saw God as my only hope, I felt it through my entire being. As Paul said, "I am fully persuaded!" My relationship with God has become deeper, richer.*   *~ Trish*

God Uses Suffering to Reorient Us and Remind Us

Amid the busyness of life, we are often blinded to what is important or what God is trying to show us. Our focus is on temporal things, and we often forget that there is another dimension to life. Suffering has a way of getting our attention like nothing else does. Everything that consumed all of our time and all the goals we thought were so important now seem inconsequential.

During this time of depression it is extremely tempting to look inward and become absorbed with what's wrong with yourself and with your life. I hope by now you have learned that as difficult as it is to peel our eyes away from our own inadequacies and failures or our troubling circumstances, we can choose to look up and talk with God in a way we might not have before.

The apostle Paul said that the weight of his hardships almost crushed him, but he was saved from despair by keeping his eyes on an eternal perspective (2 Corinthians 4:8-10,16-18). Peter also reminds us that when we suffer in our body, it actually helps us detach ourselves from temporal pleasures, become more focused on spiritual realities, and live for more eternal purposes (1 Peter 4:1-3).

When God allows hardship and suffering in our lives, we are tempted to doubt his goodness and love for us. As human beings we *do* live in clock time and our suffering, although small in comparison to eternity, seems too big and too hard to endure right now. God understands this as Jesus himself suffered in clock time. Therefore, we can rest assured that he knows and sympathizes with our tendency to doubt him during these times (Hebrews 4:14-16).

> *I feel my depression made me closer to God, and my depression was part of God's plan to draw me closer to him.*　　　　　　*-- Judy*

> *I am completely in love with him and want to serve him with all my heart. I trust him now and that makes all the difference. I no longer feel abandoned.*　　*-- Stacy*

> *I am closer to God because I feel like I draw strength from him when I need it most.*　　　　　　*~ Pam*

God Uses Suffering to Train Us

My dog, Allie, has learned a wonderful lesson that her predecessor, Rosy, never grasped. Allie quickly realized that if she obeyed me and stayed in our yard, she could have three acres to explore to her heart's content. Rosy was always chained to a post because I could not trust her to stay. We loved Rosy and dreaded the thought of losing her or finding her dead on the road. I didn't keep Rosy chained up to punish her but to protect her from her own foolishness. Had I been able to train her, she would have experienced more freedom.

When God permits suffering in our lives, we often interpret this to mean *God is punishing me for something I've done wrong.* Another more helpful and theologically accurate way of looking at these moments is that God is training us. He is not angry with us, nor does he punish us for our sins. Christ took all of God's wrath and our punishment on the cross (Colossians 1:13,19-22). God's discipline trains us so that we might learn to live the way he intends: for our good, and for his glory.

The Bible says that Jesus learned obedience in the things that he suffered (Hebrews 5:8). If Jesus was taught obedience through suffering, then we should not be surprised that God teaches us the same lessons. In my own life, battling depression has trained me to exercise self-control over my runaway emotions, to teach my mind the truth, and to take every thought captive to the obedience of Christ. To be sure, this is much, much easier to do preventively when we're not weighted down with depression. However, just as regular physical exercise helps your body stay stronger, even when you get ill, spiritual, mental, and emotional exercises train your heart (your mind, emotions, and will) to stay God-centered, even while depressed.

Be encouraged. If God trains you, it is because you are his child and he dearly loves you (Hebrews 12:5-10). Just as a loving mother would train her child to have good manners, do her homework, clean up after herself, and treat others with respect so that her child grows up to be a healthy, happy, responsible adult, God trains you. Who you are becoming and how you live your life deeply matter to him. The Bible encourages us when it reminds us, "No discipline seems pleasant at the time, but painful. Later on, however, it produces a harvest of righteousness and peace for those who have been trained by it" (Hebrews 12:11).

Spurgeon wrote:

> Stars may be seen from the bottom of a deep well when they cannot be discerned from the top of a mountain: so are many things learned in adversity which the prosperous man dreams not of. We need affliction, as the trees

need winter, that we may collect sap and nourishment for future blossoms and fruit.[7]

The Lord has used my depression to further develop my character, but sometimes I still give in to my thorn in the flesh too readily and easily.   *~Audrey*

Before I became depressed I used to try to deal with things on my own. I have realized that things are not going to change because I want them to or try to change them. The situation is in God's hands, and I have to really try to lean on him and be on my knees praying more.
          ~Shelly

I have learned to let go. I've learned that God is a God of joy.   *~Audrey*

I have learned to trust God more to use everything for his purposes.   *~Lynne*

I have realized the importance of taking my thoughts captive to Christ. I am more aware of the ways that my thinking can deteriorate and more aware of my need to seek God for his perspective. I am growing in my recognition of my need to be dependent on God with my emotions and thinking.   *~Gwen*

God Uses Suffering to Display the Reality of Who He Is to Others

One of the most influential women in my life is Joni Eareckson Tada, who was paralyzed in a diving accident when she was only 17 years old. I have followed her story, read her books, and listened to her speak since I was in college, almost 30 years ago. God uses Joni's life to show me, as well as thousands of others, the reality of Christ's mercy, love, and grace. It's not hard to praise God when everything in your life is going well. It's another story to continue to praise God and give him thanks when your life falls apart. That gets people's attention, and they sit up and take notice. What is the secret to this person's joy and peace? It's not natural. That's right. It's God.

There are only certain individuals whom God trusts with such deep suffering. Joni is one of them. Job was another. Satan thought Job's relationship with God was too shallow to endure the harsh blows of great loss, but Satan was wrong. Job continued to worship and praise God, although everything he cared about was stripped away (Job 1:20-21). Spurgeon put it best. He said,

> Any fool can sing in the day. When the cup is full, man draws inspiration from it; when wealth rolls in abundance around him any man can sing to the praise of a God who gives a plenteous harvest…It is not natural to sing in trouble…Songs in the night come only from God; they are not in the power of man.[8]

Perhaps you are one whom God trusts with his severe mercy. If so, our world desperately needs to see God in you. May you continue to hang on to him, even in the midst of your depression. Then you will be like one the Lord speaks of when he says, "In those days ten men from all languages and nations will take firm hold of one Jew by the hem of his robe and say, 'Let us go with you, because we have heard that God is with you'" (Zechariah 8:23).

Our suffering is never meaningless or purposeless. That reality gives hope to the hopeless, strength for those who are weak, and value and meaning for the one who feels worthless. Seeing God's purposes at work *in us* reminds us and encourages us that we are children of the Most High God and we are deeply cherished and valuable to him.

Learning to Be a God-Centered Woman

What we love, what we fear, and what breaks our heart say something about who we are and what's important to us. How we choose to live our lives gives us a clue as to what we believe to be true, good, and right. A Christian is not someone who holds right doctrine or theological beliefs. Living faith is in a person, Jesus Christ, not merely in a set of principles or in a doctrine of beliefs, although the right beliefs (truths) are crucial to a life well lived (2 Timothy 3:16-17). Knowledge of God is meant to bring us into intimacy with God. A true Christian is someone who is growing in their personal relationship with God, loving and trusting him while learning to live the kind of life Jesus called us all to live.

To be sure, this maturity takes a lifetime, but even in our deepest darkness, when suffering under great duress, God wants us to know him and gives us strength so that we can center ourselves in him. Thomas Kelly, in his wonderful book *A Testament of Devotion,* says,

> Life is meant to be lived from a Center, a divine Center. Each one of us can live such a life of amazing power and peace and serenity, of integration and confidence and simplified multiplicity, on one condition—*that is, if we really want to.*

Kelly continues,

> There is a divine Abyss within us all, a holy Infinite Center, a Heart, a Life who speaks in us and through us to the world. We have all heard this holy Whisper at times. At times we have followed the Whisper, and amazing equilibrium of life, amazing effectiveness of living set in. But too many of us have heeded the Voice only at times. Only at times have we submitted to his holy guidance. We have not counted this Holy Thing within us to be the most precious thing in the world. We have not surrendered *all else,* to attend to it alone.[9]

Audrey and Cheryl are learning how to center themselves in God. Listen to what they share:

> *I spend several hours per week in worship mode, either on my face or standing, in church, in my car, or at home.*

The effects of this cannot be discounted. It is a tremendous release to just get bare before the Lord, tell him your fears, and have him answer you in wisdom and in truth. There is nothing quite like it, and I could not live without my deep relationship with the Lord. If I were to stop spending time with God, I know I'd get depressed again quickly. Now, when I feel bad, I take the bad feeling to the cross and nail it there. ~Audrey

Reading and rereading God's Word has given me insight about God's reasons for allowing this sort of suffering into my life. It may sound strange, but I am beginning to view depression as more of a gift that God intends to use in my life. He has used it to strengthen my faith and trust in him. He is building endurance, patience, and compassion in me. He is forcing me to face my deepest hurts and greatest fears and to allow him to bring about healing in my heart. My prayer life has improved.

God has shown me how he intends to use my ultra-sensitivity to understand and encourage others. I have learned that tears are not evil and that hugs can be reassuring. I have learned to reject lies and to cling to truth. I now believe that God is always with me, even when it does not feel like it.

I am learning to rely on his faithfulness, love, and mercy. Hope that does not disappoint is only produced in relationship to him. I feel that in my past I was held captive by this affliction of depression that has no pity. But Jesus, who is all-loving, was sent to free the captives, and I am learning to live like a free daughter of Christ and not a bond slave chained to my emotions. God is good and everything he does is good. He never changes and his mercies are new every morning. Great is his faithfulness. ~Cheryl

The apostle Peter says we have a living hope—a big picture that helps us to endure suffering with joy because we are anticipating an extreme transformation. This profound change not only makes us unbelievably beautiful, but also pleases and glorifies God (1 Peter 1:1-9). Peter tells us that because we are aware of the eternal implications, we are to prepare ourselves mentally, emotionally, behaviorally, and spiritually. Part of preparing ourselves for eternity is accepting that suffering is part of our time while here on earth.

Thinking Through Our Pain

Something to Think About

James gives us a clue to how we build this eternal mindset when he tells us to "consider" it pure joy when we face trials (James 1:2). That means he wants us to *think* about our sufferings serving a larger purpose in our life. It may be so that we can serve others better. It may be to strengthen us. It may be to teach us some important lesson.

Are you willing to surrender your immediate goal of feeling better for a higher goal of being used by God in a significant way? If so, then perhaps that knowledge will give you hope and joy if God tarries and doesn't heal your depression as quickly as you'd like him to.

Take a minute to pray and ask God to give you that willing heart. Even our willingness is something God helps us with. Paul says, "For it is God who works in you to will and to act according to his good purpose" (Philippians 2:13).

Something to Do

Write down in your journal ways you have seen God use past difficulties in your life for a good purpose, either in your own life or in the life of someone else. If this is too difficult to see right now, look at other people you know who have experienced depression or other problems to see how God has used these problems in their lives to mature them or soften them or allow them to demonstrate the reality of God.

Sometimes, when my faith is weak, I read stories of other believers, such as Charles Spurgeon, who loved God and trusted him even through their depression. This often helps my own faith grow.

Recently I read a story about Hudson Taylor, a missionary who brought Christianity to mainland China. After he lost his wife and several children through illness, sorrow weighed heavily on his heart. To comfort and calm himself, he would pace back and forth in his study, singing softly the hymn, *"Jesus! I am resting, resting in the joy of what Thou art. I am finding out the greatness of Thy loving heart."*[10]

God wants to show you too the greatness of his loving heart. Sit quietly for a little while, breathing in and out as you learned to do in chapter 2. Place your open palms on your lap face down. When you feel relaxed, gather your worries, sorrows, confusion, doubts, fears, anger, or despair and imagine yourself letting them go for now, symbolized by your open hand, palm down. Release all these things to God. Don't rush. Let everything go, even if only for this moment.

When you're done, turn your hands over and lay them on your lap, palm side up. Receive what God has for you today. Sit quietly and let your inner heart see and hear what God wants to tell you. Before you get up, take a moment and read this encouragement from God out loud, substituting your name in the blank space.

"Dear _____, don't despair. Your GOD is present among you, a strong Warrior there to save you. Happy to have you back, he'll calm you with his love and delight you with his songs" (Zephaniah 3:17 MSG).

Earlier in the book (chapter 4), I described depression like being lost in a dark cave with no map to help you find your way out. Now you have a map. You probably will need to refer to it again and again as you work your way out of this darkness. As you do so, take a moment and look around. Ask God to open the eyes of your heart so that you might see, even in your darkness, a special gift he has for you. See, there on the floor of your dark cave, tucked in the corner, is something precious. Stoop down, scoop it up, and hold it close to you, for God promises you, "I will give you treasures hidden in the darkness—secret riches. I will do this so you may know that I am the LORD, the God of Israel, the one who calls you by name" (Isaiah 45:3 NLT).

May you come to cherish the secret treasures God gives you during your darkest times.

Scripture Verses to Help You

The following are some verses to turn to when you're feeling depressed, anxious, or lonely and unsure of the next step. Try reading them out of a paraphrase or a different translation, such as *The Message* or The New Living Translation, to hear God's Word in a fresh way. Pick a few verses and say them aloud or put them on index cards to carry with you.

When You're Afraid

Deuteronomy 1:29-30; Psalm 56:3-4; Psalm 62:1-2; Isaiah 12:2; Isaiah 44:8; Jeremiah 1:8; Nahum 1:7; Matthew 10:31; Mark 5:36; John 14:27; Philippians 4:6; 1 Peter 5:7

When You Feel Guilty and Need Forgiveness

Nehemiah 9:17; Psalm 51:1-7; Psalm 86:5; Psalm 103:2-4, 8-14; Psalm 130:4; Lamentations 1:20; Daniel 9:9; Matthew 26:28; Luke 5:21; Luke 6:37; Romans 8:1; Colossians 1:13-14; Hebrews 8:12; 1 John 1:5-9

When You Feel Overwhelmed

Psalm 4:1; Psalm 9:9-10; Psalm 16:7-9; Psalm 37:7; Psalm 55:16-17,22; Psalm 144:1-2; Isaiah 43:1-3; Matthew 26:38; Romans 12:21

When You Feel All Alone

Deuteronomy 33:27; Psalm 25:16-18; Psalm 27:10; Psalm 68:6; Psalm 73:25-26; Psalm 142:4-5; Isaiah 42:16; Isaiah 58:11; John 8:12; John 14:6; Ephesians 1:6; Hebrews 13:5

When You Need to See How God Sees You

Psalm 41:1-3; Psalm 72:12-13; Psalm 139:1-4; Psalm 147:3; Psalm 149:4; Isaiah 46:4; Isaiah 49:13,16; John 1:12; Romans

8:16,26; 2 Corinthians 6:16; Ephesians 1:4; 2 Thessalonians 2:13; 1 Peter 2:9; 1 John 3:1

When You Feel Like Giving Up
Psalm 10:14,17; Psalm 18:28; Psalm 22:24; Psalm 29:11; Psalm 61:1-4; Psalm 84:5; Psalm 119:50,92; Isaiah 43:19; Jeremiah 31:3; Romans 12:12; 2 Thessalonians 3:5

When You Feel Worn Out
Genesis 18:14; Psalm 18:6; Psalm 59:16-17; Psalm 62:5-8; Psalm 119:28; Isaiah 40:29-31; Isaiah 63:9; Jeremiah 32:17; Matthew 11:28

When You Need Hope
Psalm 30:2-3; Psalm 71:20; Psalm 119:81; Psalm 147:11; Jeremiah 29:11; Lamentations 3:21-23; Naham 1:7; John 10:10; Romans 15:13; 2 Corinthians 1:5; Philippians 4:13,19

When You Need to Know Truth
Psalm 25:4-5; Psalm 26:3; Psalm 40:11; Psalm 43:3; Psalm 86:11; Psalm 119:25,30,32,105; Proverbs 3:7-8; Isaiah 55:8-9; Jeremiah 6:16; John 8:31-32; 2 Thessalonians 2:13; 2 Timothy 3:16; 2 Peter 1:12

When You Need to Know God's Love for You
Deuteronomy 7:13; Psalm 31:7,21; Psalm 36:10; Psalm 86:13,15; Psalm 90:14; Psalm 100:5; Psalm 130:7; Isaiah 40:11; Isaiah 54:10; Jeremiah 31:3-4; John 15:9; Romans 5:5,8; Romans 8:31-39; Ephesians 3:17-19; 1 John 3:1; 1 John 4:9

When You Need to Trust God More
Psalm 9:10; Psalm 13:5; Psalm 25:1-2; Psalm 52:8; Psalm 55:23; Psalm 56:3; Psalm 73:25-26; Psalm 91:1-2; Psalm 112:7; Psalm 118:8-9; Psalm 143:8; Proverbs 3:5-6; Isaiah 8:17; John 12:36; John 14:1; Romans 15:13

When You're in Conflict with Someone
Psalm 34:14; Psalm 133:1; Proverbs 12:20; Proverbs 14:30; Proverbs 16:7; Matthew 5:23-24; Matthew 18:21-22; Romans 12:10-21; 1 Corinthians 7:15; 1 Corinthians 14:33; Colossians 3:15; 1 Thessalonians 5:13; 2 Timothy 2:24; Hebrews 12:14; James 3:18

When You Need Perspective
Psalm 39:4-5; Psalm 90:12; Proverbs 23:23; Romans 8:18, 31-37; 2 Corinthians 5:7; 2 Corinthians 12:9-10; Philippians 1:19-22

When You Need to Rejoice in the Lessons God Gives Us
Psalm 51:8,12; Psalm 66:16-20; Psalm 119:67; Psalm 126:3-5; John 16:22-24; Romans 5:2-5; 1 Thessalonians 5:16-18; 1 Peter 1:6-9

When You Need to See Purpose
Psalm 66:10: Psalm 119:71; Psalm 139:16; Isaiah 61:1-4; Romans 8:28-29; 2 Corinthians 1:9; Philippians 1:6,12-13; Ephesians 2:10; Hebrews 13:20-21; 1 Peter 5:10-11

When You Need to Experience Joy
Psalm 4:7; Psalm 16:11; Psalm 19:8; Psalm 21:6; Psalm 30:11-12; Psalm 34:8; Psalm 43:4; Psalm 118:13-14; John 15:11; Acts 14:15-17; Romans 14:17; Romans 15:13; Galatians 5:22; James 1:2

When You Need to Know Who You Are
Psalm 139:13-16; Isaiah 43:6-7; Romans 8:14-17; 1 Corinthians 10:31; Ephesians 1:4-13,17-19; 1 Peter 2:9

When Satan Is Attacking You
Matthew 6:13; John 10:10,27-29; John 17:15; 2 Corinthians 11:14; Ephesians 6:10-18; 2 Thessalonians 3:3; 1 Peter 5:8-9; 1 John 5:18-20; Revelation 12:10

Resources for Depression

Not all of these phone numbers or websites are sponsored by Christian organizations, so please use discretion when seeking help and information from them.

Finding a Christian Counselor or Physician
American Association of Christian Counselors: www.aacc.net

American Association of Pastoral Counselors: www.aapc.org

Christian Association for Psychological Studies: www.caps.net

Christian Medical and Dental Associations: www.cmdahome.org

Medication-Related Information
Drug Digest: www.drugdigest.org
    Offers information on medication and side effect comparisons.

Medical Help InfoSource: www.mhsource.com
    Offers an "Ask the Expert" feature. Although this site is geared
    for professionals and is technical, you can read the answers and
    gain some information on your particular condition.

WebMD: www.webmd.com

PharmWeb: www.pharmweb.net

Dr. Koop: www.drkoop.com

General Information About Depression
Christian Depression Pages: www.Christian-depression.org

National Institute of Mental Health: www.nimh.nih.gov

National Mental Health Association: www.nmha.org

Psych Central: psychcentral.com

Dr. Ivan's Depression Central: www.psycom.net/depression.central

American Psychological Association's Help Center:
    www.apahelpcenter.org

Mayo Clinic: www.mayoclinic.com

A Lighthouse with Healthcare Solutions for those seeking Christian acute inpatient or residential rehab for addictions and depression: www.lighthousesolutions.us or 866-890-2273.

Lighthouse Network: www.lighthousenetwork.org drbenzio@lighthousenetwork.org

Women's Issues, Menopause, Pregnancy, and Postpartum
The National Women's Health Information Center: www.4woman.gov

Women and Depression: www.psycom.net/depression.central.women

Postpartum Support International: www.postpartum.net Information and support for postpartum issues. If you don't have access to a computer, their phone number in California is (805) 967-7636.

Depression After Delivery, Inc.: www.depressionafterdelivery.com This site provides support, information, education, telephone consultation, and referrals for women and families coping with mental health problems both during pregnancy and afterwards. Their toll-free phone number for information by mail is (800) 944-4773.

Suicide Help and Prevention
Suicide Hotline: (800) 784-2433; 24-hour hotline

Suicide Prevention: (800) 827-7571; 24-hour hotline

National Suicide Hotline: (888) 248-2587; 24-hour hotline

New Hope: www.newhopenow.org or (714) 639-4673 Provides live or online Christian support with trained volunteers.

American Suicide Foundation
Provides support for family members of suicide victims (800) 531-4477.

Alternative Medicine Information
WholeHealthMD: www.wholehealthmd.com

Prevention: www.prevention.com

American Institute of Homeopathy: www.homeopathyusa.org

National Center for Homeopathy: www.homeopathic.org

Sample Letter
to Family or Friends

The support of family and friends is crucial to your recovery. Most of the time people want to help, but they don't understand what you're going through or what to do. Here is a sample letter you can give your loved ones. Feel free to modify what doesn't apply or to add things you want to say more personally.

Dear _____,

I know you've noticed I'm not myself lately and have asked what's wrong and how you could help me. I am battling depression. Here are some things I think you could do that would encourage me during this time.

- Please don't judge me. I judge myself mercilessly. I don't know why I feel the way I do, but I'm trying to figure it out. Please show patience and support.

- Please don't tell me just to "snap out of it." I don't like feeling this way. Believe me, if I could just snap out of it, I would have done so.

- Don't tell me it's all in my head. My heart hurts too. My body feels lousy, and often I feel as if I don't even have the strength to put one foot in front of another. When you say things like this, it's like telling someone who is bleeding by the side of the road, "It's all in your head. Just snap out of it."

- Speaking of bleeding by the side of the road, remember the story Jesus told of the Good Samaritan? He helped the wounded man and demonstrated compassion. Please understand that right now I may not be able to do for myself what I once was able to do. I may need your help and some of your time, energy, and/or money to get better. Please offer them generously; don't make me ask or beg. I probably won't. When you seem reluctant or unwilling to help me, I don't feel I'm worth anything to you.

- I need encouragement and support. I need you to reach out to me and not allow me to continue to isolate myself. Call me. Invite me for a walk. Come over to my house to talk with me. Don't take my reluctance or even a no for an answer. I need you right now. Pray with me and hold me. Hugs can bring more comfort than words can express. Let me cry when I need to.

- Please tell me the truth, but speak it with grace and love. I am a prisoner of my own harsh words. I do not need to hear scolding words from others. The Bible tells us to help the weak (1 Thessalonians 5:14). Right now I'm weak. Help me regain my strength. Your words are very powerful to me, especially negative ones. I hear them much louder than any other words you will ever say.

- If I'm under medical care or seeing a counselor, please understand that my doctor and/or my therapist are here to help me figure out what's wrong and how to get better. If you tell me what you think is wrong or what I should or shouldn't do to get better, it confuses me and undermines my confidence in the helpers that God has put in my life.

- Finally, in the Bible there was a man named Job who was very depressed. His friends said all the wrong things to him. Listen to his advice to them. He said,

> Won't you ever stop your flow of foolish words? What have I said that makes you speak so endlessly? I could say the same things if you were in my place. I could spout off my criticisms against you and shake my head at you. *But that's not what I would do. I would speak in a way that helps you. I would try to take away your grief* (Job 16:3-5 NLT, emphasis added).

Speak to me in a way that helps me. Encourage me. Remind me of the good things in my life. Help me trust God with all of this. Stand by me and tell me you love me, and then with your help and God's I will be able to have the strength to fight to get healthier and stronger.

Thank you for wanting to help me and caring about me. I appreciate you.

Love,

_____

How to Find
a Christian Counselor

When to Seek Outside Help

Prolonged depression is not something to ignore. If your symptoms are impairing your ability to function at home or work, or if you're having extremely negative or suicidal thoughts, you need to seek professional help immediately. Call your family physician to get a checkup and to discuss the possibility of antidepressant medication. In addition to that, I would encourage you to make an appointment with a Christian counselor so that you can begin to work on the things in your life that have contributed to you becoming depressed.

If your depression has not significantly impaired your ability to function but you have no joy in life, it's time to consider making an appointment with a counselor. God may be leading you to work on some of the issues or patterns in your life that make you depression prone in the first place. Remember, we all need loving connections and the community of others to get well and stay healthy. Counseling may be part of God's plan for your growth and well-being.

What to Look for in a Counselor

The most important thing to look for is a good fit between yourself and your potential counselor. You must feel comfortable, safe, and understood. The best way to find a good counselor is to ask others who have gone to one and received help.

Another way to find a Christian counselor is to call several churches and ask what counselor they refer people to. If you hear one or two names mentioned repeatedly, try those counselors first. If their schedule is full and they are not able to take you right away, they often will give you the names of other counselors that they work with and trust.

Your doctor may also want to give you the name of a counselor to whom he or she refers patients. Your insurance company may have names of counselors they partner with to provide counseling services to their subscribers.

When you make your initial phone call, it is very appropriate to ask some questions, such as:

- What are your fees per session?
- Do you take my medical insurance?
- What is your experience in working with depression?
- What are your professional credentials?
- Do you have a Christian orientation, and do you incorporate that into your counseling?
- Can I make an initial appointment for a consultation?

That last question gives you the option to go and check them out to see if you feel comfortable with and able to open up to this person. If for any reason after you have your first appointment you feel uncomfortable, you do not have to reschedule another appointment.

Here are some tips from women when asked what they found most helpful and most negative in their counseling experiences:

What were the things you found most helpful from your counselor?

> *Being able to express my thoughts and feelings. Being heard. Talking about my past and receiving hope for the future. Being questioned about why I think the way I do and receiving a different perspective.*   *~Stacy*

> *My counselor really listened to me.*   *~Kim*

I had a Christian counselor, and she validated me and my feelings and helped me work through my problems.
~ Maxine

It was a safe place to share anything I wanted to say and know for sure it was confidential (such a rare thing these days, confidentiality!). At times I felt the counselor was trying to take me down his path to wellness, but for the most part, he allowed me to gain resources to go on my own path through the grief and on to wholeness and happiness.
~ Melissa

Godly wisdom, a listening empathetic ear, loving correction of flawed thinking, making me consider and answer hard questions. It was not something I always looked forward to, knowing it would bring up pain, but I left knowing it was needful and good for me. ~ Gina

It was good to talk to an objective person who was really listening to me and could help me. She didn't condemn me or bring up Scripture or Christian cliches. She gave me insight into the root of my feelings and helped identify ways I could improve my situation. She suggested helpful resources. Her gentleness and kindness was appreciated.
~ Karen

It was very helpful to have my feelings validated, especially about how I saw some of my marital problems. It was reassuring to have confirmation from a neutral third party that some of my husband's attitudes and behaviors are not healthy and not emotionally supportive of me.
·- Wendy

The things that were most helpful were that she was a Christian, she set boundaries with me, she could be reached in an emergency, and she let me do the work but walked alongside me.   *~ Laura*

My relationship with God has progressed because of the therapy I received for my depression. I don't know if my relationship with God would have been rejuvenated without encouragement from my therapist. If I had gone to a "regular" counselor, I do not think I would have been directed toward God, and I don't think I would have made the progress toward normalcy that I made as a result of God's help.   *~ Donna*

My counselor has been telling me that my thoughts are not crazy.   *~ Sharon*

I had a counselor who helped me visualize things and bring Jesus into the pain I felt. I was able to talk, but he gave practical advice on how to handle things, or scripts of what to say to family to help get through tough spots. Also, my husband had gone a time or two with me, and the counselor really liked him and kept on affirming my relationship with him, which was very helpful.
~ Vikki

During the worst part of the depression prior to taking the medication, the things that were helpful in counseling were affirmation that I was not going insane, respect, lack of criticism, and patience with the confusion and mood swings. At that point, the only real support I had was the counselor I was seeing, and just her weekly presence and respect kept me from totally giving up on life.
~ Gwen

I have been in counseling off and on for years. I have learned that finding a Christian counselor that "fit" is the number one priority.   *~ Sarah*

What was the most negative aspect of your counseling experience?

> The psychiatrist I saw was secular. His suggestions were not that helpful. The first Christian counselor I saw just told me to suck it up and be submissive.   ~Lois

> Sometimes I would leave the session thinking I didn't say anything right and feeling very discouraged. I would think that everything the counselor said was right, as though she could read my mind. I didn't realize that I needed to correct her wrong assumptions. Most of the time I agreed with her because I didn't know how I felt. I had blocked out so many feelings and memories that I was just numb.   ~Sue

> Crossing of professional boundaries and the therapist trying very hard to have me see things his way.   ~Edie

> I found counseling difficult because I was telling all of my problems to a person I didn't know. The first day was particularly embarrassing because I cried almost the entire time in front of a total stranger.   ~Donna

> I went to the counselor our insurance would pay for and didn't find it helpful at all. He had no answers for me.   ~Kim

> One counselor I saw was not particularly supportive of medication and told me that depression was spiritual only.   ~Audrey

> When I went to a secular counselor, all he wanted to do was medicate me.   ~Rebekah

My counselor made me feel like if I didn't jump through her hoops she would give up on me. She showed favoritism toward my husband. She turned to work with him if I didn't or couldn't do what she wanted me to. And that increased my depression.   *~Julie*

Being misdiagnosed was very harmful to me because I was manipulated into believing something that just wasn't true and it wasted several years of my life.
                                        ~Kim

Through our church I found a husband-and-wife team and have seen the man a few times. The counselor liked to cross his legs and then uncross them and say, "Change. It's as simple as that." I was banging my head against the wall wondering why I couldn't have enough faith, enough trust, and enough courage to shake myself out of depression.   *~Sarah*

Learning to be honest about who you are and how you feel is essential to your emotional, mental, and spiritual well-being. If you're not in affirming relationships that are characterized by honesty, respect, caring, and warmth, it may take you some time to feel comfortable in the counseling relationship. Give yourself some time to feel secure. It may be just what you need to grow and learn the skills that will enable you to better connect with others in your life.

Notes

Walking out of Darkness into Light

1. NMHA.org fact sheet.

2. Valerie Davis Raskin, *When Words Are Not Enough: The Women's Prescription for Depression and Anxiety* (New York, NY: Broadway Books, 1997), p. 11.

3. Jean Baker Miller, M.D., and Irene Pierce Stiver, Ph.D., *The Healing Connection* (Boston, MA: Beacon Press, 1997), p. 16.

4. In the truest sense, a relationship with oneself is not possible because a real relationship requires a significant other. However, we do experience a love/hate relationship with ourselves, we are self-reflective, and we engage in self-talk, and those factors are significant, especially for one who is depressed.

Chapter 1—What Is Happening to Me?

1. Michael R. Lyles, M.D., "The Effects of Untreated Depression," *Christian Counseling Today,* 2002, Vol. 10, No. 4, pp. 70-71.

2. Carol Joy Cole, "Practical Guide to DSM IV Diagnosis and Treatment," *Bipolar Disorders,* 1996, p. 73.

3. Dallas Willard, *Renovations of the Heart* (Colorado Springs, CO: NavPress, 2002), p. 122.

Chapter 2—What Causes Depression?

1. Richard O'Connor, Ph.D., *Undoing Depression* (New York, NY: Berkley, 1997), p. 8.

2. David J. McKay, "Uncovering Emotion, Finding the Feelings Behind Depression," *Christian Counseling Today,* Fall 1995, p. 25.

Chapter 3—My Body: Friend or Foe?

1. Raskin, *When Words Are Not Enough,* pp. 248-49.

2. Joannie M. Schrof and Stacey Schultz, "Melancholy Nation," *U.S. News & World Report,* March 8, 1999, p. 60.

3. Archibald Alexander, *Thoughts on Religious Experience* (Carlisle, PA: The Banner of Truth Trust, 1844, 1967, 1978), p. 39.

4. Diana Schwarzbein, M.D., and Nancy Deville, *The Schwarzbein Principle: The Truth About Losing Weight, Being Healthy, and Feeling Younger* (Deerfield Beach, FL: Health Communications, Inc., 1999), p. 39.

5. See *The Schwarzbein Principle,* chapter 4, for a more thorough explanation of the brain's chemistry and how poor nutritional habits can lead to depression and how to eat healthier.

6. "Anti-Depression Foods That Keep You Thin!" *Fitness,* October 2004, p. 144.

7. Janet Holm McHenry, *PrayerWalk: Becoming a Woman of Prayer, Strength, and Discipline* (Colorado Springs, CO: WaterBrook Press, 2001), p. 15.

8. David Servan-Schreiber, "Run for Your Life," *Psychotherapy Networker,* July/August 2004, p. 50..

9. Ibid., p. 50.

10. Francois Fenelon, *Christian Perfection,* trans. Mildred Whitney Stillman (Minneapolis: Bethany House Publishers, 1975), p. 98.

11. Raskin, *When Words Are Not Enough,* p. xvi.

12. Barry Duncan, Scott Miller, and Jacqueline Sparks, "Exposing the Mythmakers," *Psychotherapy Networker,* March/April 2000, pp. 27-28.

13. Michael D. Yapko, *Breaking the Patterns of Depression* (New York, NY: Doubleday, 1997), p. xvii.

14. Personal correspondence with Karl Benzio, M.D.

15. Jay Lebow, "Reassessing SSRIs," *Psychotherapy Networker,* September/October 2004, p. 87.

16. Ibid. p. 87.

17. Jennifer Wolff, "Hooked on Antidepressants," *SELF,* July 2004, pp. 137-48.

18. David B. Biebel, Harold G. Koenig, *New Light on Depression* (Grand Rapids, MI: Zondervan, 2004), p. 206.

19. Archibald Hart, Ph.D. and Catherine Hart Weber, Ph.D., *A Woman's Guide to Overcoming Depression* (Grand Rapids, MI: Fleming H. Revell, 2007), ch. 9.

Chapter 4—Understanding Myself

1. Charles Spurgeon, *Joy in Your Life* (New Kensington, PA: Whitaker House, 1998), p. 125.

2. Wayne Grudem, *Systematic Theology* (Grand Rapids, MI: Varsity Press, 1994), ch. 23.

3. *NIV Bible, Tenth Anniversary Edition* (Grand Rapids, MI: Zondervan Publishing House, 1995), p. 783.

4. Terry Wardle, *Healing Care, Healing Prayer: Helping the Broken Find Wholeness in Christ* (Orange, CA: New Leaf Books, 2001), p. 138.

5. Yapko, *Breaking the Patterns of Depression,* p. xvii.

6. Viktor Frankl, *Man's Search for Meaning* (New York: Simon & Schuster, 1959/ 1962/1984), p. 5.

7. Dallas Willard, *Renovations of the Heart* (Colorado Springs, CO: NavPress, 2002), p. 153.

8. Thomas Kelly, *A Testament of Devotion* (New York, NY: Harper & Brothers, 1941), p. 25.

Chapter 5—The Enemy Within

1. For more on self-image and self-esteem, see chapter 1 in my book *How to Find Selfless Joy in a Me-First World* (Colorado Springs, CO: WaterBrook Press, 2003).

2. Cindy Crosby, *By Willoway Brook: Exploring the Landscape of Prayer* (Brewster, MA: Paracletc, 2003), pp. 93-94.

3. M. Scott Peck, M.D., *The Road Less Traveled* (New York, NY: Simon & Schuster, 1978), p. 58.

4. C.S. Lewis, *The Weight of Glory* (Grand Rapids, MI: Eerdmans, 1975), p. 411.

5. God's love does not rule out his judgment or his discipline. His lavish love and grace is given to bring us to repentance (see Romans 2:4-8).

6. David Powlison, *Seeing with New Eyes* (Phillipsburg, NJ: P & R Publishing Co., 2003), p. 170.

Chapter 6—Hope for When Life Becomes Too Hard

1. Alexander, *Thoughts on Religious Experience,* p. 37.

2. Kenneth S. Kendler, M.D., Ronald C. Kessler, Ph.D., Michael C. Neale, Ph.D., Andrew C. Heath, D. Phil., and Lindon J. Eaves, Ph.D., D.Sc., "The Prediction of Major Depression in Women," *The American Journal of Psychiatry,* August 1993, pp. 1139-48.

Chapter 7—Redeeming the Past

1. Judith Herman, M.D., *Trauma and Recovery* (New York, NY: Basic Books, 1992), p. 108.

2. Spiros Zodhiates, Th.D., ed., *The Complete Word Study New Testament* (Chattanooga, TN: AMG Publishers, 1991), p. 955.

3. Herman, *Trauma and Recovery,* p. 103.

4. Gary Thomas, *Seeking the Face of God* (Nashville, TN: Nelson, 1994), p. 73.

5. Fenelon, *Christian Perfection,* p. 186.

Chapter 8 —I Feel All Alone

1. Richard O'Connor, Ph.D., *Undoing Depression* (New York, NY: Berkley, 1997), p. 158.

2. www.nimh.nih.gov/publicat/depwomenknows.cfm.

3. Raskin, *When Words Are Not Enough,* p. 9.

4. C.S. Lewis, *The Problem of Pain* (New York, NY: MacMillan, 1962), p. 40.

5. For a more thorough discussion on the difference between unconditional love and conditional relationship, see chapter 7 in my book *How to Find Selfless Joy in a Me-First World* (Colorado Springs, CO: WaterBrook, 2003).

6. For more information on how to handle difficult marriage situations, see my book *How to Act Right When Your Spouse Acts Wrong* (Colorado Springs, CO: WaterBrook, 2001).

Chapter 9— Working Through Conflict

1. The Bible talks about many different kinds of desires, good and godly desires as well as sinful, unruly, selfish, and evil desires. These sinful desires are best confessed as sin, not expressed or endorsed as good.

Chapter 10—Connecting with God

1. A.W. Tozer, *Knowledge of the Holy* (New York, NY: HarperCollins, 1961), p. 35.

2. Richard Baxter, "The Cure of Melancholy and Overmuch Sorrow, by Faith," www.puritansermons.com/baxter/baxter25.html.

3. To understand more about idolatry in our heart, see chapter 4 in my book *How to Live Right When Your Life Goes Wrong* (Colorado Springs, CO: WaterBrook, 2000).

4. Rick Warren, *The Purpose-Driven Life* (Grand Rapids, MI: Zondervan, 2002), p. 17.

5. J.I. Packer, *Knowing God* (Downers Grove, IL: InterVarsity Press, 1973), pp. 14-15.

6. W.E. Vine, *Vine's Complete Expository Dictionary of Old and New Testament Words* (Nashville, TN: Thomas Nelson, Inc., 1984, 1996), p. 166.

7. L.M. Miles, "Let Me Not Doubt," copyright © 1995, used with permission.

Chapter 11—How Long, Lord, How Long?

1. Joni Eareckson Tada, Steven Estes, *When God Weeps* (Grand Rapids, MI: Zondervan Publishing House, 1997), p. 56.

2. Elizabeth Ruth Skoglund, *Bright Days, Dark Nights* (Grand Rapids, MI: Baker Books, 2000), p. 63.

3. Oswald Chambers, *My Utmost For His Highest* (1935; reprint, Uhrichsville, Ohio: Barbour, 1963), November 5.

4. Kelly, *A Testament of Devotion*, p. 71.

5. Warren, *The Purpose-Driven Life*, p. 247.

6. Skoglund, *Bright Days, Dark Nights*, p. 78.

7. Ibid., p. 78.

8. Ibid., p. 84.

9. Kelly, *A Testament of Devotion*, p. 116.

10. Dr. and Mrs. Howard Taylor, *Hudson Taylor's Spiritual Secret* (Chicago, IL: Moody Press, n.d.), pp. 208-09.

Acknowledgments

I am deeply grateful to all the women who generously shared their stories and lives with me during some of their darkest hours. I hope you know that you were heard and valued. It is my prayer that other women will find comfort and healing as they read your very personal words and that they will discover that they are not alone in their journey out of depression.

Writing a book is always a team effort. I write the words, but countless others bathe me in prayer and offer their encouragement, wisdom, support, and feedback. I could not have written this book without them.

I want to especially thank the people who regularly pray for me. I am quite sure that it was your faithful prayers and intercessions on my behalf that kept me going. I also want to express my deep appreciation to Glenna Dameron, Georgia Shaffer, Christopher Zang, Gabrielle Long, Erin Stephens, and my pastor, Howard Lawler, who read through the first draft and gave graciously of their time and expertise. Thank you, Zirka Haliby, M.D., for checking my medical facts and my assistant, Marg Hinds, for running to the library again and again and for keeping me from losing everything.

Six courageous women who battle depression agreed to read through my manuscript and offer their feedback. Stacy, Brenda, Theresa, Wendy, Gwen, and Sue, please know that your comments were invaluable. Thank you from the bottom of my heart for giving so selflessly of your time, perspective, and wonderful encouragement.

To my adult children: Ryan, thanks for cooking, cleaning up after me, and pulling all the weeds in the garden while I was writing. Amanda, your phone calls and your cheery support always brought a smile to me. You both mean the world to me. To my husband, Howard, thank you for how you always affirm the gifts God has given me and are my biggest cheerleader. I could not do what I do without you.

Harvest House, thank you for pursuing me for this project. I pray that our combined efforts will bring hope and healing to many women.

God, we both know that the conception, formation, and birthing of this book was nothing less than a miracle from you. Thank you for giving me the honor of knowing and serving you.

About the Author

Leslie Vernick is a licensed clinical social worker with a private counseling practice near Allentown, Pennsylvania. She is the author of *How to Live Right When Your Life Goes Wrong, How to Act Right When Your Spouse Acts Wrong,* and *How to Find Selfless Joy in a Me-First World.* She has also contributed to the *Soul Care Bible, Competent Christian Counseling,* and numerous other books. She is an active member of the American Association of Christian Counselors and teaches in three of their video series: *Caring for Teens God's Way, Marriage Works,* and *Extraordinary Women.* Leslie also writes a column answering relationship questions in *Today's Christian Woman.*

Leslie and her husband, Howard, have been married for more than 30 years and are the proud parents of two grown children, Ryan and Amanda.

Leslie is a popular speaker at conferences, women's retreats, and couples' retreats. She loves to encourage and motivate people to deepen their relationship with God and others. For more information on Leslie's work and ministry, visit her website at www.leslievernick.com.

~Also by Leslie Vernick ~

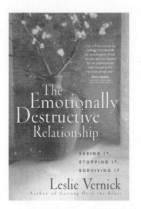

The Emotionally Destructive Relationship
Seeing It, Stopping It, Surviving It

Stop. Dare to ask the question: *What's going wrong in this relationship?*

Maybe it doesn't seem to be "abuse." No bruises, no sexual violation. Even smiles on the surface. Nonetheless, before your eyes, a person is being destroyed emotionally. Perhaps that person is someone you want to help. Perhaps it's you.

Step by step, author and counselor Leslie Vernick guides you on how to…

- recognize behaviors that are meant to control, punish, and hurt
- confront and speak truth when the timing is right
- determine when to keep trying and when to shift your approach
- get safe and stay safe
- continue to be transformed by God

Do you want to change? Within the pages of this book, you will find biblically sound, straightforward help to take the first step today.

*To read a sample chapter of this or any other Harvest House book,
go to www.harvesthousepublishers.com.*

Knowing the Heart of the Father
Four Experiences with God That Will Change Your Life
David Eckman

"David Eckman is a man you can trust...His teaching resonates with God's wisdom and compassion."
—**Stu Weber,** author of *Tender Warrior* and *Four Pillars of a Man's Heart*

You're stuffed full of Christian information. But where is God in all of it? Perhaps Christianity seems irrelevant to where your heart is really at. Maybe you're thirsting for a felt experience of the Bible's truth. What if you could...

1. have an all-encompassing sense that you have a loving heavenly Dad?

2. have a sense of being enjoyed and delighted in by Him?

3. recognize that He sees you differently than you see yourself?

4. realize that who you are is more important to Him than what you do?

These four experiences are integral to biblical Christianity. Discover what stands in the way of them, and how you can begin to know the heart of the Father in a deeper way as He works these realities into your life.

Do you want things to be different? See how these four great heart/soul transformations result in a vibrant, living faith that can stand up to the tests of life.

To read a sample chapter of this or any other Harvest House book, go to www.harvesthousepublishers.com.